SRA Prescriptive English

A Grammar, Usage, and Mechanics Intervention Program

Helps struggling students incorporate English language conventions into their writing

- **72** one-page lessons at each level review and reinforce the **key skills** that students need for **accurate writing**.

- **5** levels A-E can be used with **remedial students** from grade 3 to adult.

- **Explicit, consistent,** and **systematic instruction** ensures that all holes are filled.

- Specific lessons focus on **individual skills** to promote transfer of skills to writing.

- **Student Edition** includes all 72 lessons and review lessons.

- **Teacher's Edition** provides answers and background information.

- **Rule Booklet** includes all the English language conventions in a handy reference.

Play Catch-Up

Ideal for struggling students, each book addresses skills covered in the previous two grade levels to enable students to catch up with the rest of the class. The six units at every grade level provide comprehensive coverage of specific areas of the language arts:

- Grammar
- Usage
- Mechanics
- Reference Skills
- Vocabulary
- Writing Structure

- **Every lesson focuses on one specific skill** for explicit instruction.
- **Titles** describe the lesson skill to establish focus.
- **Rules** and **Examples** are clearly identified for ease of understanding.
- **Directions are consistent** and easy-to-follow so students always know what to do.
- **Practice exercises** provide specific and appropriate practice of the targeted skill.

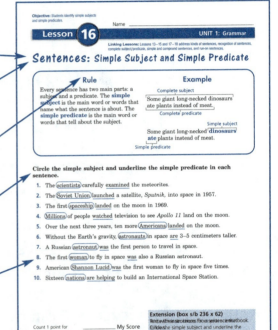

Review

Frequent unit and cumulative reviews maintain skill levels.

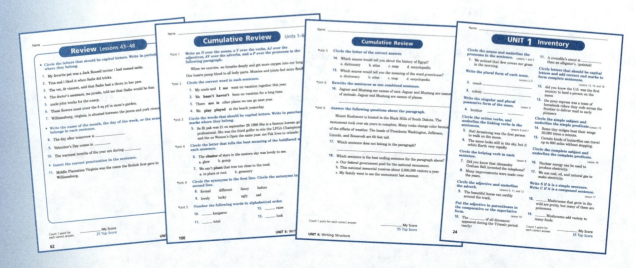

SRA Prescriptive English

Teacher's Edition

A Basic Skills Program

A Division of The McGraw·Hill Companies

Columbus, Ohio

Credits

Formerly published as *Individual Corrective English* by Edith H. Price, Flora B. Miller, and Mabel Ketterman.

Cover Photo: Eclipse Studio

www.sra4kids.com

SRA/McGraw-Hill
A Division of The McGraw-Hill Companies

Copyright © 2002 by SRA/McGraw-Hill.

All rights reserved. Except as permitted under the United States Copyright Act, no part of this publication may be reproduced or distributed in any form or by any means, or stored in a database or retrieval system, without the prior written permission of the publisher, unless otherwise indicated.

Send all inquiries to:
SRA/McGraw-Hill
8787 Orion Place
Columbus, OH 43240-4027

Printed in the United States of America.

ISBN 0-07-568960-X

2 3 4 5 6 7 8 9 QPD 06 05 04

Table of Contents

Scope and Sequence ix
How to Use This Book xiii
Professional Development
    Grammar, Usage, Mechanics, and Writing xv
    The English Language xvi
    Common Errors in Grammar, Usage, and Mechanics xvii
Diagnostic Test Blackline Master xx
Final Test Blackline Master xxi
Answer Keys xxii

UNIT 1 Grammar

		Page	Top Score
Lesson 1	Nouns	1	20
Lesson 2	Nouns: Plurals	2	20
Lesson 3	Nouns: Possessives	3	10
Lesson 4	Pronouns	4	10
Lesson 5	Verbs	5	15
Lesson 6	Adjectives	6	20
Review	Lessons 1–6	7	35
Lesson 7	Sentences: Kinds	8	10
Lesson 8	Sentences: Recognizing	9	15
Lesson 9	Sentences: Subject and Predicate	10	20
Lesson 10	Sentences: Completing	11	10
Lesson 11	Sentences: Writing	12	10
Lesson 12	Sentences: Run-Ons	13	10
Review	Lessons 7–12	14	20
Cumulative Review		15	50
Inventory		17	25

UNIT 2 Usage

		Page	Top Score
Lesson 13	Articles	18	15
Lesson 14	Contractions	19	10
Lesson 15	Pronouns: Subject Pronouns	20	10
Lesson 16	Pronouns: Object Pronouns	21	10
Lesson 17	Pronouns: Possessives	22	10
Lesson 18	Pronouns: Using *I* and *Me*	23	5
Review	Lessons 13–18	24	25
Lesson 19	Subject-Verb Agreement: *Am/Is/Are*	25	10
Lesson 20	Subject-Verb Agreement: *Was/Were*	26	10
Lesson 21	Subject-Verb Agreement: *Isn't/Aren't*	27	10
Lesson 22	Subject-Verb Agreement: *Wasn't/Weren't*	28	10
Lesson 23	Subject-Verb Agreement: *Doesn't/Don't*	29	10
Lesson 24	Subject-Verb Agreement: *Has/Have, Hasn't/Haven't*	30	10
Review	Lessons 19–24	31	10
Lesson 25	Verbs: Present Tense	32	10
Lesson 26	Verbs: Regular Past Tense	33	10
Lesson 27	Verbs: Irregular Past Tense	34	10
Lesson 28	Verb Forms: *Came/Come*	35	10
Lesson 29	Verb Forms: *Saw/Seen*	36	10
Lesson 30	Verb Forms: *Did/Done*	37	10
Review	Lessons 25–30	38	10
Lesson 31	Verb Forms: *Went/Gone*	39	10
Lesson 32	Verb Forms: *Ran/Run*	40	10
Lesson 33	Verb Forms: *Ate/Eaten*	41	10
Lesson 34	Verb Forms: *Gave/Given*	42	10
Lesson 35	Double Negatives	43	10
Lesson 36	Adjectives: Comparing	44	10
Review	Lessons 31–36	45	15
Cumulative Review		46	30
Inventory		48	20

Table of Contents

UNIT 3 Mechanics

Page | Top Score

Lesson	Title	Page	Top Score
Lesson 37	Capitalization: The Beginning of a Sentence	49	10
Lesson 38	Capitalization: Common and Proper Nouns	50	15
Lesson 39	Capitalization: Persons and Pets	51	20
Lesson 40	Capitalization: The Word *I*	52	10
Lesson 41	Capitalization: Relatives	53	10
Lesson 42	Capitalization: Months	54	10
Review	Lessons 37–42	55	20
Lesson 43	Capitalization: Days of the Week	56	10
Lesson 44	Capitalization: Holidays	57	25
Lesson 45	Capitalization: Places	58	25
Lesson 46	Punctuation: Commas in Place Names	59	15
Lesson 47	Capitalization and Punctuation: Book and Story Titles	60	20
Lesson 48	Capitalization and Punctuation: Titles	61	20
Review	Lessons 43–48	62	35
Lesson 49	Capitalization and Punctuation: Abbreviations and Initials	63	20
Lesson 50	Capitalization and Punctuation: Addresses	64	35
Lesson 51	Punctuation: Dates and Time	65	20
Lesson 52	Capitalization and Punctuation: Letters	66	10
Lesson 53	Punctuation: Commas in a Series	67	25
Lesson 54	Punctuation: Quotations	68	20
Review	Lessons 49–54	69	45
Cumulative Review		70	65
Inventory		72	60

			Page	Top Score
UNIT 4	**Vocabulary**			
Lesson 55	Word Meaning from Context		73	10
Lesson 56	Multiple-Meaning Words		74	5
Lesson 57	Synonyms		75	15
Lesson 58	Antonyms		76	15
Lesson 59	Homophones—*To, Too, Two*		77	10
Lesson 60	Homophones—*There, Their, They're*		78	10
Review	Lessons 55–60		79	10
Cumulative Review			80	70
Inventory			82	15
UNIT 5	**Reference Skills**			
Lesson 61	Alphabetical Order		83	10
Lesson 62	Using a Dictionary		84	5
Lesson 63	Reference Sources		85	5
Lesson 64	Using a Table of Contents and an Index		86	5
Lesson 65	Outlines		87	5
Lesson 66	Reading a Map		88	5
Review	Lessons 61–66		89	10
Cumulative Review			90	70
Inventory			92	15
UNIT 6	**Writing Structure**			
Lesson 67	Opening Sentences		93	10
Lesson 68	Supporting Sentences		94	10
Lesson 69	Staying on Topic		95	5
Lesson 70	Ending Sentences		96	5
Lesson 71	Sentence Order		97	10
Lesson 72	Combining Sentences		98	5
Review	Lessons 67–72		99	10
Cumulative Review			100	60
Inventory			102	15
Review List			103	
United States Postal Service State Abbreviations			105	
Index			106	

Scope and Sequence

*Numbers refer to lesson numbers.

	Skill	Book A	Book B	Book C	Book D	Book E
GRAMMAR	**PARTS OF SPEECH**					
	Nouns					
	Identifying	1	1	1	1	1, 12
	Plural	2–3	2	2–3	2–3	2
	Possessive		3	4	4	3
	Pronouns					
	Identifying	4	4	5	5	4
	Verbs					
	Action	5	5	6	6	12
	Be			7	7	12
	Helping			8	8	6, 12
	Linking			6	6	12
	Principal Parts					5
	Verb Phrases				8	6
	Adjectives					
	Comparative/Superlative	35–36	36	10	11	9
	Identifying	6	6	9, 12	9, 12	12
	Adverbs					
	Comparative/Superlative				11	9
	Identifying			11, 12	10, 12	12
	Prepositions					
	Identifying					11, 12
	Prepositional Phrases					11
	Conjunctions					
	Identifying					10, 12
	Interjections					
	Identifying					10, 12
	FUNCTIONS					
	Direct Object					7
	Indirect Object					8
	Predicate		9	15–16	15–16	16
	Subject		9	15–16	15–16	15
	SENTENCES					
	Completing	7	10			
	Kinds	9–11	7	13	13	13
	Recognizing	8	8	14	14	14
	Run-On	12	12	18	18	18
	Simple/Compound			17	17	17
	Subject/Predicate		9	15–16	15–16	15–16
USAGE	**NOUNS**					
	Adjective Agreement	13				
	Plurals and Possessives			39	40	
	PRONOUNS					
	Case (Choosing)	14–15	15–18	19–20	19–20	20–21
	Demonstrative			23	24	26
	Object	15	16	19–20	19–20	21

ix

Scope and Sequence

*Numbers refer to lesson numbers.

	Skill	Book A	Book B	Book C	Book D	Book E
USAGE	Possessive	16	17	5, 21	21	4
	Redundancies	17		24	23	24
	Reflexive			22	22	25
	Speaking of Yourself Last	18	18	19	19	20–21
	Subject	14	15	19–20	19–20	20
	Who/Whom					23
	VERBS					
	Contractions	19	14	25	25	19, 22
	Dangling Participles					31
	Double Negatives	20	35	37	26	38
	Subject-Verb Agreement					
	Be	25–28	19–22	26–28	27–28	28–29
	Be with *There*			28	28	29
	Collective Nouns				37	30
	Do		23	29	29	28
	Have	29	24	30	30	28
	Intervening Phrases					30
	Tense/Form of Verbs					
	Choosing Tense	21				
	Future Perfect					
	Past or Past Participle (Choosing):					
	Ate/Eaten		33	34	31	32
	Began/Begun				36	35
	Blew/Blown					36
	Broke/Broken				34	34
	Came/Come	30	28	35	31	33
	Chose/Chosen				34	34
	Did/Done	32	30	35	32	33
	Drank/Drunk				36	32
	Drew/Drawn					36
	Drove/Driven				33	
	Flew/Flown					36
	Froze/Frozen					35
	Gave/Given		34	34	31	34
	Grew/Grown				35	36
	Knew/Known			36	35	36
	Ran/Run			32	36	32	35
	Rang/Rung				36	32
	Rode/Ridden					34
	Sang/Sung				36	32
	Sank/Sunk					32
	Saw/Seen	31	29	36	32	33
	Spoke/Spoken				34	34
	Stole/Stolen					35
	Swam/Swum					32

Scope and Sequence

*Numbers refer to lesson numbers.

Skill		Book A	Book B	Book C	Book D	Book E
USAGE	Threw/Thrown				35	36
	Took/Taken			34	31	33
	Tore/Torn				33	35
	Went/Gone	33	31	35	32	33
	Wore/Worn				33	35
	Wrote/Written				33	34
	Present	21–22	25	31		
	Problem Verbs:					
	Bring/Take					40
	Lie/Lay					39
	May/Can			40	39	40
	Sit/Set			40	39	39
	Simple Past (irregular)	24	27	33	38	27
	Simple Past (regular)	23	26	32		
	ADJECTIVES					
	Articles: A/An	34	13	38	39	
	Choosing			41–42	41–42	41
	ADVERBS					
	Choosing			41–42	41–42	41
	Good/Well, Bad/Badly			42	42	41
	PREPOSITIONS					
	Choosing					42
MECHANICS	**CAPITALIZATION**					
	Beginning of Sentence	37	37	14	14	14
	Book, Song, Story, Poem Titles		47	50	46	47
	Common/Proper Nouns	39	38		44	43
	Days of the Week	44	43	47	47	44
	Holidays	45	44	50	47	44
	I	41	40	43	43	44
	in Letters	53	50, 52	49	51	51
	Months	43	42	47	47	44
	Nationalities				49	46
	Organizations				44	46
	Persons and Pets	40	39	43	43	44
	Places	46, 49	45	46	48	46
	Relatives	42	41	44	43	
	Seasons				47	
	Titles of People	48	48	44	46	45
	Words Made from Countries				49	46
	PUNCTUATION					
	Abbreviations	47	49	45	45	45
	Apostrophes		3, 14	4, 39	4	3
	End Marks	38	7	13	13	13
	in Letters	53	52	49	51	51
	Quotations	54	54	51	52	54

xi

Scope and Sequence

*Numbers refer to lesson numbers.

	Skill	Book A	Book B	Book C	Book D	Book E
MECHANICS	Semicolons					48
	Time	52	51			
	Commas					
	Appositives					53
	Coordinating Conjunctions			54	53	52
	Dates	52	51	48	50	49
	Direct Address			53	50	50
	Introductory Words			53	50	50
	Place Names	50	46	48	48	49
	Series		53	52	50	49
	Subordinate Clauses				54	52
VOCABULARY	Analogies					60
	Antonyms	59	58	57	57	56
	Compound Words	56				
	Homophones	60	59–60	59–60	58, 59	57
	Multiple-Meaning Words	57	56	58		58
	Rhyming	55				
	Synonyms	58	57	56	56	56
	Word Context		55	55	55	55
	Word Roots				60	59
REFERENCE SKILLS	Alphabetical Order	61	61	61	61	
	Charts			66		
	Dictionary	62	62	62	62	61
	Graphs			66		
	Indexes	65	64	64	63	62
	Maps	66	66	63	66	
	Outlines		65	66	64	
	Reference Sources	63	63	65	65	63
	Research					66
	Tables					65
	Tables of Contents	64	64	64	63	62
	Webs					64
WRITING STRUCTURE	Combining Sentences	72	72	72	70	72
	Completing Paragraphs	68				
	Ending Sentences	71	70	70		
	Main Idea/Topic Sentence	67	68	67	67	67
	Opening Sentences			67		
	Paragraphs				71	70
	Paragraphing Quotations				72	71
	Sentence Order	70	71			69
	Staying on Topic	69	69	69	69	69
	Supporting Sentences	68	68	68	68	68

Prescriptive English

. . . is a comprehensive program that teaches and reviews basic language arts skills. The series is designed to support any language arts basal or to stand alone for independent review and reinforcement.

What skills are covered in Prescriptive English?

The skills are organized into six units.

❶ Grammar

Grammar refers to the names and functions of the parts of the speech. It involves the development of a common vocabulary when discussing issues of language use.

❷ Usage

Usage is the way language is actually used. Once students have the basic terminology for grammar, they can think about and discuss usage in an intelligent way. They will have the building blocks for using their language in a way that is accepted in society as standard English.

❸ Mechanics

Mechanics are the technical rules for the language. These include capitalization and punctuation.

❹ Vocabulary

Vocabulary skills are those skills that help students build their word knowledge and help them discover the relationship of words and their parts.

❺ Reference Skills

Reference skills are those skills that help students find and organize information.

❻ Writing Structure

Writing structure refers to the underlying structure and organization of paragraphs and compositions.

Classroom Management

- The seventy-two lessons can be completed at a rate of two per week.
- The lessons can be used by individual students for practice and remediation or by classroom groups.
- The lessons are self-directing and allow students to work independently after minimal introduction by the teacher, if necessary.
- The lessons can be assigned sequentially, or the teacher can diagnose areas of weakness by administering the unit Inventory before assigning the lessons in each unit. Students who need remediation can then be assigned the appropriate lessons in that unit.
- The teacher can refer to the Scope and Sequence on pages ix–xii to correlate the skills to any language arts basal program.

Overview

Lesson Features

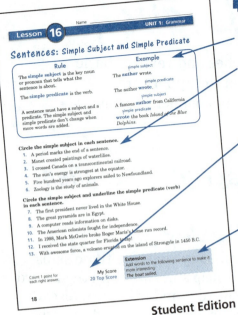

Student Edition

- **Rule Box** provides clear rules and examples.
- **Practice** Consistent, easy-to-follow exercises provide an opportunity for students to apply the rules learned in the lesson.
- **Scoring** A place for the student's score and an indication of the top score for each lesson provide a daily record of progress. Top scores are always in multiples of 5 for easy calculation.
- **Extension** An extension activity suggests additional practice using the skills in speaking or writing.

Teacher's Edition

- **Objective** gives a clear goal for the lesson.
- **Linking Lessons** relates lesson skills to one another.
- **FYI** provides additional information, facts, and instruction tips.

Program Features

- **Scope and Sequence**
  These pages provide a complete matrix of skills covered at all levels.

- **Diagnostic and Final Tests**
  Blackline masters help place students and test their knowledge of language arts skills.

- **Inventories**
  These tests can be given to diagnose particular problems or as a unit test.

- **Reviews**
  A review lesson is provided after every six lessons to provide practice for specific skills.

- **Cumulative Reviews**
  At the end of each unit, the Cumulative Review provides integrated practice for skills covered from the beginning of the book.

- **Student Reference Material**
  Review List provides a brief reference for the language arts skills covered in the book.
  Postal Abbreviations can be used with the mechanics lessons on letters or for general reference.
  Proofreading Marks can be used to introduce students to a consistent method for correcting their work.

Grammar, Usage, Mechanics, and Writing

Writing is a complicated process. It requires the combination of handwriting, spelling, vocabulary, grammar, usage, genre structures, and mechanics skills with ideas to create readable text. Many students never progress beyond speech written down, writing down what they say as they would say it. Mature writers, however, take composition beyond conversation. They understand the importance of audience and purpose for writing. They organize their thoughts, eliminating those that do not advance their arguments and elaborating on those that do, so that their readers can follow a logical argument or story. Mature writers also know and appreciate the conventions of grammar, usage, spelling, and mechanics. They proofread and edit for these conventions, so their readers are not distracted by errors.

The Study of English Conventions

Over the years, the study of grammar, usage, and mechanics has gone in and out of favor. As far back as ancient Greece, the study of grammar was seen as a fundamental area of study. Mathematics and grammar have also been linked as studies in logic. Grammar is also tied to prestige and socio-economic status. Upper class dialects with differences in pronunciation, structure, and vocabulary tend to define the traditional English conventions.

In the past century, much research has been done to demonstrate the effectiveness of traditional types of instruction in the conventions of English. Experience and research have shown that learning grammatical terms and completing grammar exercises has little effect on the way students use language. These skills do not play a significant role in idea generation or the prewriting and drafting phases of the writing process. In fact, emphasis on correct conventions has been shown to have a damaging effect when it is the sole focus of writing instruction. If students are evaluated only on the proper use of spelling, grammar, and punctuation, they tend to write fewer and less complex sentences.

Knowledge of English conventions is, however, vitally important in the editing and proofreading phases of the writing process. A paper riddled with mistakes in grammar, usage, or mechanics is quickly discounted. Many immature writers never revise or edit. They finish the last sentence and turn their papers in to the teacher. Mature writers employ their knowledge of English language conventions in the editing phase to refine and polish their ideas.

The study of grammar, usage, and mechanics is important for two reasons.

1. Educated people need to know and understand the structure of their language, which in large part defines their culture.
2. Knowledge of grammar gives teachers and students a common vocabulary for talking about language and makes discussions of writing tasks clearer and more efficient.

The key issue in learning grammar, usage, and mechanics is how to do it. On the one hand, teaching these skills in isolation from writing has been shown to be ineffective and even detrimental if too much emphasis is placed on them. On the other hand, not teaching these skills and having students write without concern for conventions is equally ineffective. The answer is to teach the skills directly in the context of their importance in the editing phases of the writing process. Students should be taught proper use of punctuation or subject/verb agreement at the same time they are taught to proofread for those conventions. Correcting errors is an editorial skill rather than a composing skill.

Prescriptive English *is designed to give students the tools they need to edit and proofread their work effectively. In short and direct lessons, it covers basic grammar, usage, and mechanics conventions so that students understand them and can identify correct and incorrect applications.*

Professional Development

The English Language

A basic understanding of the history and structure of the English language helps students understand the rich but complex resource they have for writing.

The History of English

● Old English

The English language began about A.D. 450 when the Angles, Jutes, and Saxons–three tribes that lived in northern Europe–invaded the British Isles. Much of their language included words that had to do with farming (sheep, dirt, tree, earth). Many of their words are the most frequently used words in the English language today.

● Middle English

In 1066 William the Conqueror invaded England and brought Norman French with him. Slowly Old English and Norman French came together and Middle English began to appear. Today 40 percent of Modern English comes from French. When the printing press was introduced, English became more widespread.

● Modern English

With the Renaissance and its rediscovery of classical Greek and Latin, many new words were created from Greek and Latin word elements. This continued intensively during the Early Modern English period. The rich language was used in the writings of Shakespeare and his contemporaries and profoundly influenced the nature and vocabulary of English. With dictionaries and spelling books, the English language became more standardized, although it continues to be influenced by other languages and new words and trends.

The Structure of English

● Grammar

Grammar is the sound, structure, and meaning system of language. People who speak the same language are able to communicate because they intuitively know the grammar system of that language. All languages have grammar and yet each language has its own grammar.

Traditional grammar study usually involves two areas: parts of speech and sentence structure or syntax. Parts of speech (nouns, verbs, adjectives, adverbs, pronouns, infinitives, conjunctions) are typically considered the content of grammar. The parts of speech involve the *form* of English words. Sentence structure (subjects, predicates, objects, clauses, phrases) involves the *function* of the parts of speech.

● Mechanics

Mechanics involves the conventions of punctuation and capitalization. Punctuation makes writing easier to read. There are about twelve puctuation marks in English. Proper punctuation involves marking off sentences according to grammatical structure. In speech students can produce sentences as easily as they can walk, but in writing they must think about what a sentence is.

● Usage

Language varies over time, across national and geographical boundaries, by gender, across age groups, and by socioeconomic status. When the variation occurs within a given language, the different versions of the same language are called dialects. Every language has a prestige dialect associated with education and financial success. In the United States, this dialect is known as Standard English and is the language of school and business.

Usage involves the word choices people make when speaking certain dialects. Word choices that are perfectly acceptable in conversation among friends may be unacceptable in writing. Usage is the most obvious indicator of the difference between conversation and composition. Errors in word usage make writers look ignorant and jeopardize their credibility. Usage depends on a child's cultural and linguistic heritage. If the dialect children have learned is not the formal language of school settings or if it is not English, children must master another dialect or language in order to write Standard English.

Common Errors in Grammar, Usage, and Mechanics

Most of the time native speakers of English use correct grammar automatically. However, there are a few mistakes that show up again and again. Most of these errors do not seriously alter a writer's meaning. They do, however, have the power to hinder or halt the average reader and cause the reader to lose respect for the writer. Correctness should not be the sole study of a language arts class, but it must be part of it as long as readers show no tolerance for errors. Awareness of the common errors that students make can help teachers and students demystify the production of Standard English. As they analyze and classify the typical mistakes students make, students can target and master those particular conventions.

● Editing/Proofreading Errors

Some of the errors students make in writing are simply the result of not carefully reading their final drafts. Many errors occur because the writer's thought train has been interrupted and a sentence is not complete or a word is skipped. Most often the writer can correct these on his or her own. A major emphasis of any English composition program should be to teach the editing and proofreading phases of the writing process so students can eliminate these types of errors.

● Punctuation Errors
- Commas at odd junctures
- Sentence fragments ending with a period or question mark
- Commas joining independent clauses
- No punctuation resulting in confused meaning or run-on sentences
- Limited use of punctuation (not using a colon to present a series, not using dashes to connect thoughts)

● Capitalization Errors

Many times capitalization errors are simply handwriting problems. Students start writing in all capital letters or randomly write capital letters, causing capital letters to appear in unusual places. The other common problem is in capitalizing words that should not be capitalized.

● Usage
- Incorrect case or tense *(lie/lay, who/whom)*
- Wrong word choice *(among/between, sit/set, less/fewer, that/which)*
- Dialect. These errors, such as "She bought me them shoes," require students to learn Standard English patterns.

● Grammar Errors

Verbs
- Verb forms, particularly irregular verb forms *(swim/swam/swum)*
- Verb tense shifts within a paragraph
- Subject/verb agreement, particularly collective nouns, such as *everyone*

Nouns
- Irregular plurals *(wolves, deer)*
- Plural *(babies)*, possessive *(baby's)*, and plural possessive *(babies')* forms

Pronouns
- Possessive forms of pronouns *(their)*
- Inappropriate pronoun case changes *(his/he, they/them)*
- Shifts in person
- Antecedent (the word to which the pronoun refers) and pronoun number agreement
- Missing antecedent (when a pronoun has no noun to which it refers)

Complex Errors

Sometimes students write sentences that raise grammatically complex problems that require understanding of grammar.

- **Faulty Parallelism.** Parts of a sentence parallel in meaning are not parallel in structure.
- **Non sequiturs.** A statement does not follow logically from something said previously.
- **Dangling Modifiers.** A phrase or clause does not logically modify the word next to it.
- **Awkwardness**. Sentences are not written simply.
- **Wordiness.** Thoughts are not written in as few words as possible.
- **Vocabulary.** Precise words are not used.

Professional Development

Objective: Students complete the Diagnostic Test to help assess their skill level.

Name _____

Diagnostic Test

Unit 1

Choose the correct answer about the parts of speech in the sentence.

The carpenter measured the boards and cut them with her new saw.

1. The sentence has _____ nouns and _____ verbs.
   a. 4, 2   b. 3, 2   c. 2, 1

Choose the possessive nouns that belong in the sentence.

2. The _____ blanket was made by _____ grandmother.
   a. babies, Thomas   b. babys', Thomas'   c. baby's, Thomas'

Choose the correct complete subject in the sentence.

The tallest existing tree is in Redwood National Park.

3. a. Redwood National Park   b. tallest
   c. The tallest existing tree   d. Park

Choose the correct complete predicate in the sentence.

The giant sequoia tree stands 365 feet tall.

4. a. 365   b. stands 365 feet tall
   c. giant sequoia tree   d. tree

Unit 2

Choose the correct word or words to complete each sentence.

5. _____ use a saw without wearing safety goggles.
   a. Don't   b. Dont   c. Don't'

6. Manuel _____ to the hardware store to get some nails.
   a. run   b. ran   c. runned

7. _____ want to build a tree house.
   a. Me and Jacob   b. Jacob and me   c. Jacob and I

8. We _____ expecting it to be so hard to make!
   a. wasn't   b. weren't   c. was

Unit 3

Choose the best answers for the underlined parts of the sentence.

On <u>tues</u> at <u>900</u> <u>uncle andy</u> came over to help us with the tree house.

9. a. tues.   b. Tues.   c. tues
10. a. 9,00   b. :900   c. 9:00
11. a. Uncle Andy   b. uncle Andy   c. Uncle andy

xviii

Diagnostic Test

Unit 4 **Choose the best meaning for the underlined word.**

I watched as Uncle Andy cut the lumber with his saw.

12. a. tool for cutting wood   b. to have seen

Choose the best synonym for the word *unsafe*.

13. a. careful   b. dangerous   c. smooth   d. bumpy

Choose the best antonym for the word *rough*.

14. a. careful   b. dangerous   c. smooth   d. bumpy

Choose the correct word to complete the sentences.

15. You can leave the extra lumber over _____.
   a. there   b. their   c. they're

16. I think _____ coming to get it tomorrow.
   a. there   b. their   c. they're

Unit 5 **Circle the letter of the correct answer.**

17. Which of these is a main topic that includes the other three words?
   a. pine   b. maple   c. trees   d. oak

18. Which of these would best tell you how to get from Denver to Chicago?
   a. dictionary   b. telephone book   c. encyclopedia   d. atlas

Choose the answer that correctly lists the words in alphabetical order.

19. a. hammer, nails, lumber, ladder
   b. nails, ladder, lumber, hammer
   c. lumber, ladder, nails, hammer
   d. hammer, ladder, lumber, nails

Unit 6 **Circle the letter that lists the sentences in correct order.**

20. 1. Next, you should pick out the lumber you will need.
   2. Building a tree house requires planning.
   3. Then, find the proper tools to cut the lumber.
   4. First, you should have some building plans.
   a. 3, 2, 1, 4   b. 2, 4, 1, 3   c. 1, 2, 3, 4

Count 1 point for each correct answer.

_____ My Score
20 Top Score

Diagnostic Test

Objective: Students are tested on the language arts skills covered in Book B.

Name _____

Final Test

Unit 1

Choose the answer that lists the correct parts of speech in the sentence.

1. The plumber fixed our broken shower.
   a. 3 nouns, 2 verbs, 1 pronoun
   b. 2 nouns, 4 verbs, 1 pronoun
   c. 2 nouns, 1 verb, 1 pronoun

Choose the possessive nouns that belong in the sentence.

2. The _____ tools helped him fix all of the _____ leaks.
   a. plumbers, pipe   b. plumbers', pipes   c. plumber's, pipe's

Choose the correct complete subject in the sentence.

The pipes in our kitchen freeze in the winter.

3. a. pipes   b. kitchen   c. The pipes in our kitchen   d. in the winter

Choose the correct complete predicate in the sentence.

Water flows through pipes.

4. a. Water   b. through pipes   c. flows through pipes   d. pipes

Unit 2

Choose the correct word to complete each sentence.

5. "Your shower _____ fixed correctly the last time," the plumber told us.
   a. weren't   b. wasn't   c. were

6. The plumber _____ us tips on how to save water at home.
   a. gave   b. given   c. gived

7. "Don't _____ really long showers," he said.
   a. took   b. takes   c. take

8. "You should _____ to turn the water off while brushing your teeth," he said.
   a. try   b. tries   c. tried

Unit 3

Choose the best answers for the underlined parts of the sentence.

"I'll need a <u>wrench a saw and new washers</u> to fix the <u>sink" the</u> plumber told us.

9. a. wrench a saw, and new washers   b. wrench, a saw and new washers
   c. wrench, a saw, and new washers

10. a. sink" the   b. sink," the   c. sink." the

Unit 4 — **Choose the best meaning for the underlined word.**

11. The hot water tank is in the basement.
  a. a heavy military vehicle   b. a container for holding liquids

12. We let the water run from the faucet to fill the sink.
  a. to flow rapidly   b. to go faster than a walk

Choose the best synonym for *peaceful*.

13. a. angry   b. smooth   c. calm

Choose the best antonym for *damaged*.

14. a. perfect   b. broken   c. better

Choose the correct word to complete the sentences.

15. Those pipes are _____ short.
  a. to   b. too   c. two

16. The ones we want to use are over _____.
  a. there   b. their   c. they're

Unit 5 — **Circle the letter of the correct answer.**

17. Which of these is a main topic that includes the other three words?
  a. wrench   b. hammer   c. pliers   d. tools

18. Which of these would list the different meanings of the word *drain*?
  a. encyclopedia   b. atlas   c. dictionary   d. newspaper

Choose the answer that correctly lists the words in alphabetical order.

19. a. powder, pipes, pressure, water
  b. water, pressure, pipes, powder
  c. pressure, water, powder, pipes
  d. pipes, powder, pressure, water

Unit 6 — **Choose the letter that lists the sentences in the correct order.**

20. 1. We called the plumber.
  2. The faucet on our sink broke.
  3. We paid the plumber and can now use our sink.
  4. The plumber came to our house and fixed it.
  a. 3, 2, 1, 4   b. 2, 4, 3, 1   c. 2, 1, 4, 3   d. 4, 2, 1, 3

Count 1 point for each correct answer.

_____ My Score
20 Top Score

Final Test

Answer Keys

Diagnostic Test

1. b
2. c
3. c
4. b
5. a
6. b
7. c
8. b
9. b
10. c
11. a
12. a
13. b
14. c
15. a
16. c
17. c
18. d
19. d
20. b

Final Test

1. c
2. c
3. c
4. c
5. b
6. a
7. c
8. a
9. c
10. b
11. b
12. a
13. c
14. a
15. b
16. a
17. d
18. c
19. d
20. c

UNIT 1

Objective: Students identify and write nouns.

Name _____

Lesson 1

Grammar

Nouns

Linking Lessons: Lesson 2 addresses plural nouns more thoroughly, and possessive nouns are covered in Lesson 3. Lesson 38 deals with capitalization of proper nouns.

Before starting this unit, you may wish to give the Inventory on page 17 as a diagnostic test.

Rule
A **noun** is the name of a person, place, or thing.

Example
person   person
John Muir was a **man** who loved

thing   thing   place
trees and **nature**. **Muir Woods**, a

thing   place
park in **California**, was named after him.

Circle the nouns in the sentences.

1. The (ground) shook in (Washington).
2. An (earthquake) caused (Mount Saint Helens) to erupt.
3. It blew (ashes) and (gases).
4. (Trees) were torn from the (soil).
5. Some (people) and many (animals) were killed.
6. (Nature) can repair itself.
7. (Plants) began to grow again.
8. (Insects), (birds), and (fish) returned.
9. (Humans) also helped restore the (area).
10. The (U.S. Forestry Service) planted (trees) and built new (roads).

Count 1 point for each correct answer.

_____ My Score
20 Top Score

Extension
Make some compound words by combining two nouns. For example, the nouns *wild* and *life* can be joined to make *wildlife*.

FYI: Explain to students that ideas or qualities, such as honesty, pride, friendship, and happiness, are also nouns.

1

Objective: Students form plural nouns with the endings -s, -es, -ies, and -ves.

Lesson 2

UNIT 1: Grammar

Linking Lessons: Lessons 19–24 address subject-verb agreement.

Nouns: Plurals

A noun that stands for more than one person, place, or thing is a **plural noun.**

Rule		Example
Add -s to the ends of most nouns to form the plural.	star	The sun is one of the **stars** in our solar system.
Add -es to nouns ending in s, x, z, ss, ch, or sh.	bus	Public **buses** help reduce pollution.
Change the y to i and add -es to nouns that end in a consonant plus y.	factory	Machines have replaced people in some **factories.**
If the final f in a word has the v sound in the plural form, change the f to v and add -es.	wolf	**Wolves** live in packs.

Write the plural form of each noun.

1. buzz _buzzes_
2. baby _babies_
3. leaf _leaves_
4. rocket _rockets_
5. donkey _donkeys_
6. brush _brushes_
7. party _parties_
8. gas _gases_
9. sky _skies_
10. scratch _scratches_
11. box _boxes_
12. calf _calves_
13. shell _shells_
14. penny _pennies_
15. wish _wishes_
16. shelf _shelves_
17. dress _dresses_
18. buddy _buddies_
19. lunch _lunches_
20. minnow _minnows_

Count 1 point for each correct answer.

_____ My Score
20 Top Score

Extension
Make up a sentence with two plural words from this page.

FYI: Musical terms that end in *o* form plurals by adding only *s* (for example, *pianos* and *concertos*). The same is true for words of Spanish origin that end in *o* (for example, *tacos* and *sombreros*).

Objective: Students identify and form singular and plural possessive nouns.

Lesson 3

UNIT 1: Grammar

Linking Lessons: You may want to review Lesson 2 on plural nouns. Possessive pronouns are addressed in Lesson 17.

Nouns: Possessives

Rule	Example
A singular possessive noun shows ownership by one person or thing.	**Sacajawea's** picture is on the gold coin.
A plural possessive noun shows ownership by more than one person or thing. To make a plural noun that ends in s possessive, add only an apostrophe.	**Polar bears'** thick coats help them survive in cold climates.
To make a plural noun that does not end in s possessive, add an apostrophe plus s.	**Women's** right to vote was approved in 1920.

Circle the possessive noun that belongs in each sentence.

1. Michael Jordan was the **Chicago Bull's** (**Chicago Bulls'**) star player.
2. *Tom Sawyer* is the **books'** (**book's**) title and main character.
3. A duplex has two (**families'**) **family's** homes in one building.
4. *Cricket* is a popular **childrens'** (**children's**) magazine.
5. A good diet is important for **everyones'** (**everyone's**) health.
6. The forest is a (**fox's**) **foxes'** favorite habitat.

Write the singular possessive and plural possessive form of each noun.

7. girl _girl's, girls'_
8. class _class's, classes'_

Extension
Write a few sentences describing what kind of clothes your friends wear. Use singular and plural possessive nouns.

Count 1 point for each correct answer. _____ My Score 10 Top Score

FYI: Students might have difficulty making the possessive forms of irregular plurals. Discuss the plural possessives *mice's*, *people's*, and *series'* and point out that the rule for adding an apostrophe only or an apostrophe plus s still applies.

3

Objective: Students identify and write pronouns.

Lesson 4

Name _____

UNIT 1: Grammar

Linking Lessons: Lessons 15–18 cover pronouns in further detail, including subject, object, and possessive pronouns.

Pronouns

Rule	Example
A **pronoun** is a word that is used in place of a noun or nouns.	Shel Silverstein wrote **his** book <u>A Light in the Attic</u> in 1981.
The pronoun has to agree with the noun it replaces. If the noun is singular, the pronoun must be singular.	A <u>frog</u> starts **its** life as a tadpole.
If the noun is plural, the pronoun must be plural.	<u>Butterflies</u> start life as caterpillars. Then **they** come out of **their** cocoons.

Circle the pronouns in the paragraph.

Sojourner Truth made a famous speech in 1851. (It) was about women's rights. Ending slavery was also important to (her). (They) were both subjects Sojourner knew about. (She) was born a slave and freed at the age of 30. Many Americans can thank brave people like Sojourner Truth for (their) freedom and rights.

Circle the correct pronoun in each sentence.

1. All of the presidents have had   his   (their)   portraits painted.
2. Babies need parents to take care of   (them)   it.
3. Amelia Earhart flew   (her)   she   airplane across the Atlantic Ocean.
4. The flashlight gets   (its)   their   energy from a battery.
5. Emily Dickinson's poems weren't published when   her   (she)   was alive.

Count 1 point for each correct answer.

_____ My Score
10 Top Score

Extension
Write a few sentences describing a person you admire.

FYI: You might want to have students identify the antecedent in these exercises as well. This will reinforce the concept of the pronoun replacing a noun or nouns.

Objective: Students identify and use action verbs.

Name _____

Lesson 5

UNIT 1: Grammar

Linking Lessons: Lessons 19–24 address subject-verb agreement. Present tense and past tense verbs are covered in Lessons 25–27. For practice with choosing the correct past tense form of specific verbs, see Lessons 28–34.

Verbs

Rule	Example
Words that name an action are called **verbs.**	Fans **cheered** when Sammy Sosa **hit** a home run.

Circle each action verb.

1. The tour guide (talked) about the history of Blarney Castle.
2. Dolphins (swim) along the coast of North Carolina.
3. Johnny Appleseed (planted) apple trees in the 1700s.
4. I (play) card games on my computer.
5. Alice McLerran (wrote) the book *Roxaboxen*.
6. Earth (rotates) around the sun.
7. George Washington Carver (discovered) new uses for peanuts.
8. Very few people (live) near the North Pole.
9. The United States (entered) World War II in 1941.
10. Bean seeds (sprout) quickly.
11. Passengers (jumped) from the *Titanic* into lifeboats.
12. The invention of airplanes (changed) transportation forever.
13. Each state (elects) a governor.
14. The Grand Canyon (runs) through Arizona.
15. The fastest horses (compete) in the Kentucky Derby.

Count 1 point for each correct answer.

_____ My Score
15 Top Score

Extension
Write about what you do every morning to get ready for school. Use at least five action verbs.

FYI: If students have trouble identifying action verbs, suggest that they ask themselves what the main person or thing in the sentence did or is doing.

Objective: Students recognize and write adjectives.

Name _____

Lesson 6

UNIT 1: Grammar

Linking Lessons: Adjectives classified as articles (*a*, *an*, and *the*) are covered in Lesson 13. Practice with comparative and superlative forms of adjectives is provided in Lesson 36.

Adjectives

Rule	Example
An **adjective** is a word that describes a noun. They can tell us **which one, what kind, what color,** or **how many**.	Ducks fly **long** distances. **Male** mallards have **green** heads.

Circle the adjectives in the sentences.

1. Zimbabwe has an (interesting) flag.
2. The flag has (seven) (bright) stripes.
3. The stripes are (green) (yellow) (red) and (black).
4. There is a (big) triangle on the (left) side of the flag.
5. Inside the triangle is an (unusual) bird on a star.
6. The triangle has a (plain) background.

Write adjectives that could describe a tree, a fish, and a playground. Choose from the words below.

noisy   tall   fun   slippery   straight   wet   shady   scaly   crowded

tree	fish	playground
tall	slippery	noisy
straight	wet	fun
shady	scaly	crowded

Count 1 point for each correct answer.

_____ My Score
20 Top Score

Extension
Add at least two adjectives to the following sentence: *The students checked out books from the library.*

FYI: You might want to remind students that an adjective can come before or after the word it describes.

Objective: Students review nouns (including plural and possessive forms), pronouns, verbs, and adjectives.

Name _____

Review Lessons 1–6

Circle the nouns in the paragraph.

The (sun) is actually a (star). It is a big (ball) of hot (gases). (Life) on (Earth) would not be possible without the (sun). Its (energy) becomes (heat) and (light).

Write the plural form of each noun.

1. fox _____foxes_____
2. branch _____branches_____
3. stripe _____stripes_____
4. shelf _____shelves_____
5. bunny _____bunnies_____
6. donkey _____donkeys_____

Write the singular possessive and plural possesive form of each noun.

	Single Possessive	Plural Possessive
7. parent	parent's	parents'
8. baby	baby's	babies'
9. doctor	doctor's	doctors'

Write a pronoun to replace each underlined noun.

10. <u>Walnuts</u> drop from trees in the fall. ___They___

11. The Medal of Honor was given to <u>Dr. Mary Walker</u> in 1865. ___her___

12. Simon Lake invented <u>the submarine</u>. ___it___

Circle the action verbs and underline the adjectives in the paragraph.

Gloria Estefan is a <u>Cuban</u> singer. She (sings) <u>wonderful</u> songs in Spanish and English. Gloria is very <u>popular</u> for her <u>enjoyable</u> concerts. She also (dances) when she (performs). Gloria (makes) her <u>loyal</u> fans very <u>happy</u>.

• Lessons 1–2 • Lesson 2 • Lesson 3 • Lesson 4 • Lessons 5–6

Count 1 point for each correct answer.

_____ My Score
35 Top Score

UNIT 1: Grammar

7

Objective: Students identify statements, questions, and exclamations and their corresponding end marks.

Name _____

Lesson 7

UNIT 1: Grammar

Linking Lessons: In Lesson 11 students write sentences, including statements, questions, and exclamations.

Sentences: Kinds

Rule	Example
A **statement** ends with a period.	Great Danes are nice dogs.
A **question** ends with a question mark.	What is your favorite kind of dog?
An **exclamation** ends with an exclamation point.	That's a very big dog!

Put a period, a question mark, or an exclamation point at the end of each sentence.

1. What color is an emerald**?**
2. A newborn horse is called a foal**.**
3. The human brain has three main parts**.**
4. When did the Civil War end**?**
5. *Babe* was the best movie I've ever seen**!**
6. Oscar Wilde was an Irish author**.**
7. The World Wide Web is part of the Internet**.**
8. Will people ever live on the moon**?**
9. We rode the most amazing roller coaster**!**
10. How cold does it get in Iceland**?**

Count 1 point for each correct answer.

_____ My Score
10 Top Score

Extension
Write your own statement, question, and exclamation. Practice the different ways you would say each one.

FYI: Exclamations can be only a word or two: Oh, my! Really! These kinds of exclamations usually express a feeling of surprise.

Objective: Students identify complete sentences and distinguish them from fragments. Students recognize that sentences always begin with a capital letter.

Name _____

Lesson 8

UNIT 1: Grammar

Linking Lessons: In Lesson 9 students identify complete subjects and predicates. Lessons 10 and 11 provide practice with completing and writing sentences. Capitalizing the beginning of a sentence is covered in Lesson 37.

Sentences: Recognizing

Rule	Example
A **sentence** makes a complete thought. A sentence always begins with a capital letter.	The piano was invented in Italy. Where was the television invented?

Write Yes before each sentence. Write No before each group of words that is not a sentence. Add the correct end marks to the sentences.

yes 1. The Beatles was a famous rock group **.**

_no_ 2. In the sixties

yes 3. How many members were in the band **?**

yes 4. All four Beatles were born in Liverpool, England **.**

yes 5. What instruments did they play **?**

_no_ 6. Played guitar and piano

_no_ 7. Recorded 18 albums in 8 years

yes 8. John and Paul wrote most of the songs **.**

_no_ 9. Many different styles

_no_ 10. Didn't think they could

Count 1 point for each correct answer.

_____ **My Score**
15 Top Score

Extension
Write three complete sentences about your favorite musical group.

FYI: Fragments are sometimes used intentionally for effect. However, that technique should be reserved for more sophisticated writers.

9

Objective: Students identify complete subjects and predicates in sentences.

Lesson 9

UNIT 1: Grammar

Linking Lessons: You may want to review Lessons 1 and 5 on nouns and verbs and Lesson 8 on complete sentences. Lessons 10 and 11 provide practice with completing and writing sentences.

Sentences: Subject and Predicate

Every sentence has a subject and a predicate. The **subject** tells *who* or *what*, and the **predicate** tells what the subject *does*, *has*, or *is*.

Rule
The **complete subject** includes all the words in the subject of a sentence. The **complete predicate** includes all the words in the predicate of a sentence.

Example
Complete Subject

Tropical rain forests have the greatest variety of plant life.

Complete Predicate

Circle the complete subject and underline the complete predicate.

1. (Plants) need air, water, and light.
2. (Not all plants) need soil.
3. (Water hyacinths) float and grow on top of water.
4. (The oldest living plant) is a pine tree in California.
5. (It) is 4,700 years old.
6. (Some trees) lose their leaves in the fall.
7. (An evergreen tree) keeps its leaves or needles all year long.
8. (The study of plant life) is called botany.
9. (Mint, sage, and basil) are all herbs.
10. (These and other herbs) can be used fresh or dried.

Count 1 point for each correct answer.

_____ My Score
20 Top Score

Extension
Add words to the following sentence to make the subject and predicate more interesting: *We bought them.*

FYI: Not all of the words in the subject or the predicate have the same importance. The main word or words in the complete subject are the *simple subject*; the main word or words in the complete predicate are the *simple predicate*.

Objective: Students identify and form complete sentences.

Name _____

Lesson 10

UNIT 1: Grammar

Linking Lessons: It might be helpful to review Lesson 8, on recognizing complete sentences, and Lesson 9, on subjects and predicates.

Sentences: Completing

Rule
Every sentence has two parts. The **subject** names the person or thing the sentence is about. The **predicate** tells something about the subject. They go together to make a complete thought.

Example
Subject
The first log cabins were built in America in Delaware.
Predicate

Circle the word group that completes each sentence.

1. The word *origami* (means "to fold paper.") a Japanese art.
2. Sound waves in outer space. (travel through the air.)
3. Many people (visit Niagara Falls.) in a boat.
4. Software programs with games to play. (tell a computer what to do.)
5. Still-life paintings (are pictures of objects.) on the museum wall.
6. The common cold and drinking juices. (lasts one to two weeks.)
7. The Nile (is the longest river.) in Egypt and Sudan.
8. E. B. White (wrote Charlotte's Web.) and an author.
9. Eyeglasses (were invented in 1290.) worn by many people.
10. One quart or two pints. (equals two pints.)

Count 1 point for each correct answer.

_____ My Score
10 Top Score

Extension
Find out what your state's flower is and write two complete sentences about it.

FYI: In most sentences, the subject comes before the predicate. However, in some sentences, such as questions, part or all of the predicate comes first.

Objective: Students write complete sentences, choosing from statements, questions, and exclamations.

Name _____

Lesson 11

UNIT 1: Grammar

Linking Lessons: It may be helpful to review Lessons 7–9 on kinds of sentences, recognizing sentences, and identifying subjects and predicates, respectively.

Sentences: Writing

Rule	Example
A **sentence** is a group of words that makes a complete thought. It may tell something, or it may ask something.	Montana's state fair is held at Great Falls. Where does Florida have its state fair?

Write a sentence using each group of words. Begin each sentence with a capital letter. Put a period, question mark, or exclamation point at the end of each sentence. The first one is done for you. **Answers will vary.**

1. to the state fair __My family went to the state fair.__
2. a lot of animals _____
3. a goat _____
4. the horses _____
5. marched in a parade _____
6. won a great prize _____
7. was fun _____
8. a big tent _____
9. drank some lemonade _____
10. awesome fireworks _____
11. we all _____

Count 1 point for each correct answer.

_____ **My Score**
10 Top Score

Extension
Write a statement, a question, and an exclamation about a fair or other special event you have attended.

FYI: Suggest that students read the sentences to themselves to help them decide what kind of end mark to use.

Objective: Students correct run-on sentences by writing separate sentences with correct capitalization and punctuation.

Lesson 12

UNIT 1: Grammar

Name _____

Linking Lessons: You might want to review Lessons 8 and 9 on recognizing complete sentences and identifying subjects and predicates.

Sentences: Run-Ons

A **run-on** sentence is two or more sentences that are incorrectly written as one sentence.

Rule
To correct a run-on, write separate sentences.

Example
The National Road took 18 years to build it brought pioneers from East to West. (incorrect)

The National Road took 18 years to build. It brought pioneers from East to West. (correct)

This paragraph is hard to understand because it has some run-on sentences. Find where each sentence begins and ends. Write in end marks and circle letters that should be capitalized.

Pioneers needed a way to send and receive news. There was not a good mail service. (A) group of men developed the pony express. The pony express was a team of horseback riders. (T)hey rode across the western United States to deliver mail. One rider handed off mail to another rider. Each rider rode about 75 miles. (M)any of the riders were teenagers. The pony express riders traveled by horse day and night. (T)hey kept riding even in bad weather. (T)heir route went from Missouri to California. It took ten days to cover the 2,000 miles.

Count 1 point for each correct answer.

_____ My Score
10 Top Score

Extension
Write a short letter to a friend or relative who lives far away.

FYI: Combining sentences is another way to correct a run-on. If students use this strategy accurately, their answers should be considered correct.

Objective: Students review kinds of sentences (including statements, questions, and exclamations), complete sentences, subjects and predicates, and run-ons.

Name _____

Review Lessons 7–12

- **Put a period, a question mark, or an exclamation point at the end of each sentence.**

  1. A cheetah can run 70 miles per hour**.**
  2. It is an amazing animal**!**
  3. How fast does a snail move**?**
  4. The dragonfly is the fastest insect**.**

• Lesson 7

- **Write Yes before each sentence. Write No before each group of words that is not a sentence.**

  5. __yes__ A rectangle has four sides
  6. __no__ How many sides does
  7. __no__ What a cube is
  8. __yes__ All four sides of a square are equal

• Lesson 8

- **Write a sentence using each group of words. Then, circle the complete subject and underline the complete predicate.**
  (Answers will vary. Three points each.)

  9. had a birthday party _____

  10. the best present _____

• Lessons 9–11

- **Find where each sentence begins and ends. Write in end marks and circle letters that should be capitalized.** (Six points total.)

  Alaska is called "The Last Frontier." (I)t is the biggest and coldest state. The capital of Alaska is Juneau. (T)wo other big cities are Anchorage and Fairbanks. Some important products from Alaska are oil, natural gas, and fish. (T)he state also produces lumber and wood products.

• Lesson 12

Count 1 point for each correct answer.

_____ My Score
20 Top Score

14　　　　　　　　　　　　　　　　　　　　　　　　　UNIT 1: Grammar

Objective: Students review cumulatively Unit 1 (Grammar).

Name _____

Cumulative Review

- Lesson 1

Circle the nouns in the sentences.

1. (Water) is a (resource) we can recycle.
2. (Rain) brings fresh (water) to (rivers) and (lakes).
3. These are (places) where most (humans) get their (water).
4. Some (factories) clean (water) for (humans) to use.

- Lesson 2

Write the plural form of each noun.

5. story ___stories___
6. boss ___bosses___
7. patch ___patches___
8. bonus ___bonuses___

- Lesson 3

Circle the possessive noun that belongs in each sentence.

9. A **yellow cobras'** (**yellow cobra's**) venom can be deadly.
10. All of the (**states'**) **state's** governors went to the meeting.
11. **Baby's** (**Babies'**) bodies have 350 bones.

- Lesson 4

Circle the pronouns in the sentences.

12. Some lizards can make (their) own tails fall off.
13. Michelle Kwan won (her) first World Championship when (she) was only 15.
14. A puffer fish can make (its) body get bigger.

- Lessons 5–6

Circle the action verbs and underline the adjectives in the paragraph.

The Wizard of Oz is a <u>popular</u> movie. In it, a tornado (carries) a girl named Dorothy into a <u>magical</u> land. She (meets) a <u>talking</u> scarecrow, a <u>tin</u> woodsman, and a <u>cowardly</u> lion.

UNIT 1: Grammar

Name _____

Cumulative Review

- Lesson 7

Put a period, a question mark, or an exclamation point at the end of each sentence.

15. Can you get a sunburn on a cloudy day**?**

16. Pluto is the smallest and coldest planet**.**

17. What a wonderful day it is**!**

- Lesson 8

Write Yes before each sentence. Write No before each group of words that is not a sentence. Add end marks to the sentences.

__yes__ 18. Many children have lived in the White House**.**

__yes__ 19. Abraham Lincoln's sons had goats**.**

__no__ 20. Raised dogs and ponies

- Lesson 9

Circle the complete subject and underline the complete predicate.

21. (People) use different kinds of energy.

22. (Solar power) comes from the sun.

23. (Using less hot water) helps save energy.

- Lesson 10

Draw a circle around the group that completes each sentence.

24. The Women's Museum   in Dallas, Texas.   (is in Dallas, Texas.)

25. Exercise   and a good diet.   (helps you feel stronger.)

- Lesson 12

Find the beginning and end of each sentence. Rewrite the sentences without run-ons. (Two points each.)

26. Maps have symbols they stand for real things and places.
Maps have symbols. They stand for real things and places.

27. A map with symbols has a key the key tells what the symbols mean.
A map with symbols has a key. The key tells what the symbols mean.

Count 1 point for each correct answer.   _____ My Score
50 Top Score

UNIT 1: Grammar

Objective: Students are assessed on their knowledge of grammar.

Name _____

UNIT 1 Inventory

Circle the nouns and underline the verbs.
Lessons 1, 5

1. (People) ski in (Colorado).

Write the plural form of each noun.
Lesson 2

2. jelly __jellies__
3. arch __arches__

Circle the correct possessive noun.
Lesson 3

4. A hurricanes' (hurricane's) winds blow over 72 miles per hour.
5. These (trees') tree's dead limbs should be trimmed.

Write a pronoun to replace the underlined noun.
Lesson 4

6. The president appoints <u>members of the Cabinet</u>. __them__

Write an adjective to describe each noun. Answers will vary.
Lesson 6

7. frog _____
8. building _____

Write Yes before each sentence and put in the correct end mark. Write No if the words are not a sentence.
Lessons 7–8

__yes__ 9. Harps are instruments.
__no__ 10. How to play it

Circle the complete subject. Underline the complete predicate.
Lesson 9

11. (Swimming and soccer) <u>are summer Olympic sports</u>.
12. (The movie *The Prince of Egypt*) <u>is one of my favorites</u>.
13. (Many people in the United States) <u>speak Spanish</u>.

Write a complete sentence using the group of words.
Lessons 10–11
Answers will vary.

14. go to the museum

_____

_____

Find where the sentences begin and end. Write in end marks and circle letters that should be capitalized.
(Five points total.)
Lesson 12

Fossils are found all over Earth. (i)n parts of Africa, fossils of early humans were found. Some insect fossils are found in amber. (a)mber is hardened tree sap. (f)ossils have also been found in ice and tar.

Count 1 point for each correct answer.

_____ My Score

25 Top Score

UNIT 2

Usage

Objective: Students identify and use *a*, *an*, and *the* correctly.

Name _____

Lesson 13

Linking Lessons: It might be helpful to review Lesson 1 on nouns.

Before starting this unit, you may wish to give the Inventory on page 48 as a diagnostic test.

Articles

A, *an*, and *the* are useful words called **articles.** They signal to a reader that a noun is coming.

Rule

A is used before a word that begins with a consonant sound. *An* is used before a word that begins with a vowel sound.

The is used with a particular person, place, thing, or idea.

Example

Doves use their beaks like **a** straw.

An owl can see at night.

The hawk spotted **the** juicy grasshopper 100 yards away.

Circle the articles in the paragraph.

(A) predator is (an) animal that eats other animals. (The) animals they catch and eat are called prey. (A) snake could be (a) mouse's predator. (An) unlucky snake might be prey to (a) hawk.

Write *a*, *an*, or *the* to complete each sentence.

1. Ostriches are __the__ biggest birds.

2. Climax, Colorado, is __the__ highest town in __the__ country.

3. Dial __the__ number 911 in __an__ emergency.

4. Sunlight is really __a__ mix of many colors.

5. __An__ anthology is __a__ collection of writing or music.

Count 1 point for each correct answer.

_____ **My Score**

15 Top Score

Extension
Write three sentences using *a*, *an*, and *the* with the following words:
umbrella   bicycle   picture

FYI: Most people vary their pronunciation of *the* for emphasis. For example, for just sharing information, you might say "The Internet is the (e pronounced with schwa sound) place to find whatever you need." However, to emphasize the usefulness of the Internet, you might say, "The Internet is *the* (e pronounced with long e sound) place to find whatever you need."

Objective: Students form and use contractions.

Name _____

Lesson 14

UNIT 2: Usage

Linking Lessons: Lessons 21–24 address subject-verb agreement with contractions formed by a verb and the word *not*.

Contractions

Rule	Example
A **contraction** is a shortened form of two words that are joined together. When the words are combined, one or more letters are left out, and an apostrophe takes their place.	are not—aren't, could not—couldn't did not—didn't, do not—don't has not—hasn't, was not—wasn't cannot—can't, will not—won't

Write a contraction from the words in parentheses.

1. Los Angeles __isn't__ the capital of California. (is, not)
2. Richard Nixon __didn't__ finish his second term as president. (did, not)
3. An orchestra __wouldn't__ be complete without violins. (would, not)
4. __Don't__ forget to write the zip code on a letter. (do, not)
5. Colds __aren't__ caused by cold weather. (are not)
6. A pig __couldn't__ outrun a cheetah. (could, not)
7. __Wasn't__ the first space shuttle called *Enterprise*? (was, not)
8. An electric car __doesn't__ need gas. (does, not)
9. Teeth that __haven't__ been brushed will get cavities. (have, not)
10. We __can't__ see the sun at night because Earth turns away from it. (cannot)

Count 1 point for each correct answer.

_____ My Score
10 Top Score

Extension
Write three contractions that are formed with the word *not*.

FYI: You might want to demonstrate to students the importance of including an apostrophe in contractions. Write *we'll* and *well* on the board and discuss the different meanings of the words.

Objective: Students choose the correct subject pronoun to replace a noun or nouns.

Name _____

Lesson 15

UNIT 2: Usage

Linking Lessons: You might want to review Lesson 4 on pronouns. Lessons 16 and 17 address object pronouns and possessive pronouns. Lesson 18 provides practice with choosing between *I* and *me*.

Pronouns: Subject Pronouns

A pronoun takes the place of one or more nouns. **Subject pronouns** are used as subjects in a sentence. Subjects are the persons or things that perform the action of the sentence.

Rule
I, you, he, she, and *it* mean only one (singular).

You, we, and *they* mean more than one (plural).

Example
I know that pearls come from oysters.

They are used to make jewelry.

Write a subject pronoun to replace the underlined noun or nouns.

1. <u>Samuel Clemens</u> was a famous American author. __He__
2. <u>You and I</u> know him as Mark Twain. __We__
3. <u>Clemens's parents</u> moved to Hannibal, Missouri, where he grew up. __They__
4. <u>The Mississippi River</u> ran beside his town. __It__
5. <u>Steamboats</u> stopped in Hannibal, and <u>Clemens</u> watched them. __They__ __he__
6. <u>Olivia Langdon</u> married Samuel Clemens in 1870. __She__
7. <u>Tom Sawyer and Huckleberry Finn</u> are two of Twain's characters. __They__
8. <u>My friends and I</u> enjoy reading Twain's books. __We__
9. <u>Ms. Ramirez</u>, our librarian, talks with us about the books. __She__

Count 1 point for each correct answer.

_____ My Score
10 Top Score

Extension
Write a few sentences about a book you like. Use at least three subject pronouns.

FYI: A subject pronoun may also be used as a predicate noun, in which case it's called a predicate pronoun.

Objective: Students choose the correct object pronoun to replace a noun or nouns.

Name _____

Lesson 16

UNIT 2: Usage

Linking Lessons: You might find it helpful to review Lesson 4 on pronouns. Lessons 15 and 17 cover subject pronouns and possessive pronouns. Lesson 18 provides practice with choosing between *I* and *me*.

Pronouns: Object Pronouns

Object pronouns follow verbs and words like *to, for, at, of,* and *with*.

Rule	Example
Me, you, him, her, and *it* mean only one (singular).	Muhammad Ali didn't think anyone could beat **him.**
Us, you, and *them* mean more than one (plural).	U.S. presidents always have Secret Service agents near **them.**

Write the correct pronoun in each sentence. Use the words in parentheses.

1. The first cars didn't have radios in __them__. (them, they)

2. What does history have to do with you and __me__? (me, I)

3. The air around __us__ is a mixture of many gases. (we, us)

4. Most colas have sugar in __them__. (them, they)

5. A queen bee lays eggs, and worker bees take care of __her__. (her, she)

6. If you cut roses, put __them__ in water right away. (they, them)

7. Elvis Presley's fans adored __him__. (he, him)

8. Mom read Arnold Adoff's poem "The Apple" with __me__. (I, me)

9. Put lemon juice on a cut apple to keep __it__ from turning brown. (them, it)

10. Checking and savings accounts are two services banks offer __us__. (us, we)

Count 1 point for each correct answer.

_____ My Score

10 Top Score

Extension
Rewrite this sentence with two object pronouns: *Rain soaked my clothes when I went out to get the newspaper.*

FYI: Object pronouns are used as direct objects, indirect objects, and objects of prepositions.

21

Objective: Students choose the correct possessive pronoun to replace a noun or nouns.

Name _____

Lesson 17

UNIT 2: Usage

Linking Lessons: It might be helpful to review Lesson 4 on pronouns. Lessons 15 and 16 cover subject pronouns and object pronouns.

Pronouns: Possessives

A pronoun takes the place of one or more nouns. **Possessive pronouns** show ownership and may take the place of a possessive noun.

Rule

My, mine, your, yours, her, hers, his, and *its* mean only one (singular).

Our, ours, your, yours, their, and *theirs* mean more than one (plural).

Example

Queen Elizabeth I tried to keep **her** country at peace.

The people of England loved **their** queen.

Choose the correct possessive pronoun for each sentence.

1. The Civil War is said to be (ours, our) country's first modern war. __our__

2. For the first time, troops traveled by train to (their, its) posts. __their__

3. An officer could get messages from (his, him) leader by telegraph. __his__

4. Reporters followed troops to get news for (theirs, their) newspapers. __their__

5. Harriet Tubman helped the North with (her, our) spying skills. __her__

6. (My, Mine) report is about Rose Greenhow and (she, her) group of spies who helped the South. __My__ __her__

7. Mathew Brady and (his, him) assistants took photographs of the war. __his__

8. The *Monitor* was a ship famous for (their, its) iron-covered hull. __its__

9. Southern leaders named (their, its) iron-hulled ship *Merrimack*. __their__

Count 1 point for each correct answer.

_____ My Score

10 Top Score

Extension
Find out more about the Civil War. Write one sentence each about the North and the South. Use a possessive pronoun in each.

FYI: Most possessive pronouns are followed by the noun that is the possession. However, the possessive pronoun *mine* can stand alone. For example, *This pencil is mine.*

Objective: Students choose correct usage of the pronouns *I* and *me*.

Name _____

Lesson 18

UNIT 2: Usage

Linking Lessons: You might find it helpful to review Lesson 15 on subject pronouns and Lesson 16 on object pronouns. Lesson 40 covers capitalization of the word *I*.

Pronouns: Using *I* and *Me*

Rule	Example
The pronoun *I* is a subject pronoun. When you tell what you and someone else did or had, use the pronoun *I*.	Carlos and **I** are going to the art museum.
The pronoun *me* is an object pronoun. When you tell what someone did to or for you and someone else, use the pronoun *me*.	Our teacher gave tickets to Carlos and **me**.
When writing about yourself and another person, you should speak about yourself last.	Incorrect An artist talked to me and Carlos. Correct An artist talked to Carlos and me.

Write *I* or *me* to complete each sentence.

1. Carlos and __I__ left early in the morning.

2. My mom dropped Carlos and __me__ off at the art museum.

3. The first thing Carlos and __I__ wanted to see was a sculpture.

4. Our teacher said Carlos and __I__ did a good job on our project.

5. She gave him and __me__ an A on our clay sculpture.

Count 1 point for each correct answer.

_____ My Score

5 Top Score

Extension
Write three sentences about yourself and someone else. Use *I* or *me* in each one.

FYI: Tell students that if they try each pronoun alone with the verb, it will be easier to identify which pronoun belongs. For example, in the first sentence, it would not be correct to say *Me left early in the morning*, so *I* must be the correct answer.

Objective: Students review articles; contractions; and subject, object, and possessive pronouns.

Name _____

Review Lessons 13–18

- Write *a*, *an*, or *the* to complete each sentence.

1. ___An___ alligator is not as fierce as a crocodile.

2. Native Americans were ___the___ first people to live in America.

- Write a contraction to complete each sentence. Use the words in parentheses.

3. A puma ___doesn't___ keep the spots it is born with. (does, not)

4. Humans ___can't___ hear as well as dogs. (cannot)

5. Lions and tigers ___shouldn't___ be kept as pets. (should, not)

- Circle the pronouns in the paragraph. Write *S* above the subject pronouns, *O* above the object pronouns, and *P* above the possessive pronouns.

(You)[S] may walk, ride a bike, or take a bus to (your)[P] school. Maybe (you)[S] ride in a car or on a train. A long time ago, people walked or rode (their)[P] horses or mules. (They)[S] also rode in wagons pulled by animals. Henry Ford thought (he)[S] could improve the way people travel. In 1908 (he)[S] started making (his)[P] famous Model T cars. People could travel faster and farther in (them)[O].

- Write *I* or *me* to complete each sentence.

6. Jenny and ___I___ love to look at butterflies.

7. Suki gave some wildflower seeds to Jenny and ___me___.

• Lesson 13
• Lesson 14
• Lessons 15–17
• Lesson 18

Count 1 point for each correct answer.

_____ My Score
25 Top Score

Objective: Students choose from *am*, *is*, and *are* and write the correct verb to agree with the subject of a sentence.

Name _____

Lesson 19

UNIT 2: Usage

Linking Lessons: Lessons 20–24 also address subject-verb agreement with various verbs.

Subject-Verb Agreement: Am/Is/Are

Rule	Example
Use **am** with the pronoun *I*.	I **am** proud of my mother.
Use **is** when you talk about one person, place, or thing.	She **is** a surgeon.
Use **are** when you talk about more than one person, place, or thing. Also use **are** with the pronoun *you*.	Surgeons **are** doctors who operate on people. **Are** you going to the hospital?

Write *am*, *is*, or *are* to complete each sentence.

1. The pathway that electricity moves through __is__ called a circuit.
2. I __am__ taking aluminum cans to the recycling center.
3. An employer __is__ someone who hires and pays people to work.
4. All rocks __are__ made of one or more minerals.
5. __Are__ tomatoes a fruit or a vegetable?
6. A pulley __is__ a simple machine.
7. Milk, cheese, and beans __are__ rich in calcium.
8. *The Golden Touch* is a myth I __am__ reading with my class.
9. Bones __are__ one of your body's fastest growing parts.
10. Next year I __am__ going to see the pyramids in Egypt.

Count 1 point for each correct answer.

_____ My Score
10 Top Score

Extension
Write about an activity you and friends have planned. Use *am*, *is,* and *are* in your sentences.

FYI: Phrases that come between a subject and verb (such as *as well as*, *except*, and *besides*) do not affect the number of the verb. If the subject is singular, a singular verb is used. For example, *Alex, as well as his sister, is going to college.*

Objective: Students choose from *was* and *were* and write the correct verb to agree with the subject of a sentence.

Name _____

Lesson 20

UNIT 2: Usage

Linking Lessons: Lesson 19 and Lessons 21–24 also address subject-verb agreement with various verbs.

Subject-Verb Agreement: Was/Were

Rule	Example
Use *was* when you talk about one person, place, or thing.	The bicycle **was** invented by James Starley.
Use *were* when you talk about more than one person, place, or thing.	Both the helicopter and the jet airplane **were** invented in 1939.

Write *was* or *were* to complete each sentence.

1. Benjamin Franklin __was__ a great American.

2. Writing and inventing __were__ things he loved to do.

3. The first book he wrote __was__ an almanac.

4. He __was__ also helpful in writing the Declaration of Independence.

5. Bifocal glasses and lightning rods __were__ two of his inventions.

6. Bifocal glasses __were__ helpful for seeing close up and at a distance.

7. The post office __was__ another idea of Benjamin Franklin's.

8. Franklin __was__ not paid for his inventions.

9. They __were__ his way of helping people.

10. Benjamin Franklin __was__ a kind and giving man.

Count 1 point for each correct answer.

_____ My Score
10 Top Score

Extension
Find out about another invention. Write three sentences about the invention using *was* and *were*.

FYI: The following compound pronouns are singular and should always have a singular verb: *anybody, everyone, someone, something, nobody,* and *nothing.*

Objective: Students choose from *isn't* and *aren't* and write the correct verb to agree with the subject of a sentence.

Name _____

Lesson 21

UNIT 2: Usage

Linking Lessons: You might find it helpful to review Lesson 14 on contractions formed with the word *not*, and Lesson 19, which addresses subject-verb agreement with the verbs *am*, *is*, and *are*.

Subject-Verb Agreement: *Isn't/Aren't*

Rule	Example
Isn't is a verb that means "is not." Use *isn't* when you talk about one person, place, or thing.	The Pacific Ocean **isn't** along the coast of Florida.
Aren't is a verb that means "are not." Use *aren't* when you talk about more than one person, place, or thing.	Oceans **aren't** made of freshwater.

Write *isn't* or *aren't* to complete each sentence.

1. Oregon __isn't__ part of the corn belt.
2. Peninsulas __aren't__ completely surrounded by water.
3. Mountains and plains __aren't__ shaped alike.
4. There __isn't__ as much water on Earth's surface as there is underground.
5. __Isn't__ Richmond the capital of Virginia?
6. Skiing and sledding __aren't__ activities you can do in a desert.
7. A creek __isn't__ as big as a river.
8. __Aren't__ the Sierra Nevada mountains in California?
9. The Black Hills __aren't__ really hills; they're mountains.
10. New York __isn't__ a state that borders Wyoming.

Count 1 point for each correct answer.

_____ My Score
10 Top Score

Extension
Write a description of your state's features. Use *isn't* and *aren't*.

FYI: The words *each*, *every*, *either*, *neither*, *one*, *another*, and *much* are always singular and require a singular verb.

Objective: Students choose from *wasn't* and *weren't* and write the correct verb to agree with the subject of a sentence.

Name _____

Lesson 22

UNIT 2: Usage

Linking Lessons: You might find it helpful to review Lesson 14 on contractions formed with the word *not*, and Lesson 20, which addresses subject-verb agreement with the verbs *was* and *were*.

Subject-Verb Agreement: Wasn't/Weren't

Rule

Wasn't is a verb that means "was not." Use *wasn't* when you talk about one person, place, or thing.

Weren't is a verb that means "were not." Use *weren't* when you talk about more than one person, place, or thing and with the pronoun *you*.

Example

Annie **wasn't** my favorite musical.

Our seats **weren't** very good.
You **weren't** with us when we saw that show.

Write *wasn't* or *weren't* to complete each sentence.

1. The people of Turkey __weren't__ prepared for the earthquake in 1999.
2. William Henry Harrison __wasn't__ president for very long.
3. Football helmets have changed because the first ones __weren't__ safe.
4. Men's names __weren't__ always used for hurricanes.
5. Women's speed skating __wasn't__ an Olympic event until 1960.
6. The dodo bird __wasn't__ able to fly.
7. Pictures on the first television screens __weren't__ in color.
8. Slavery __wasn't__ legal in the United States after 1865.
9. Scientists discovered that Tyrannosaurus Rex __wasn't__ the biggest dinosaur.
10. You didn't see the Big Dipper because you __weren't__ looking for it.

Count 1 point for each correct answer.

_____ My Score
10 Top Score

Extension
Write three sentences about a play or concert you have seen.

FYI: The words *both*, *few*, *many*, *others*, and *several* are always plural and require a plural verb.

Objective: Students choose from *doesn't* and *don't* and write the correct verb to agree with the subject of a sentence.

Name _____

UNIT 2: Usage

Linking Lessons: You might find it helpful to review Lesson 14 on contractions formed with the word *not*.

Subject-Verb Agreement: Doesn't/Don't

Rule
Doesn't means "does not." Use *doesn't* when you talk about one person, place, or thing and with *he, she,* and *it*.

Don't means "do not." Use *don't* when you talk about more than one person, place, or thing and with *I, you, they,* and *we*.

Example
Venus **doesn't** have any moons.
It **doesn't** move around the sun as quickly as Mercury.

Scientists **don't** think there could be life on Venus.
We **don't** see the sun during a total solar eclipse.

Write *doesn't* or *don't* to complete each sentence.

1. The moon __doesn't__ make any light of its own.
2. Jupiter __doesn't__ have as many moons as Saturn.
3. The outer planets __don't__ get as much heat from the sun.
4. The sun __doesn't__ revolve around Earth.
5. The orbits of Earth and Mars __don't__ cross.
6. We __don't__ know for sure if there is life on other planets.
7. An astronomer __doesn't__ do the same thing as an astrologer.
8. The moon goes through phases, but it __doesn't__ change shape.
9. Stars __don't__ last forever.
10. Astronomers __don't__ know why Jupiter's Great Red Spot changes in size.

Count 1 point for each correct answer.

_____ My Score
10 Top Score

Extension
Write a few sentences about why it would be hard to live on the moon.

FYI: Some nouns that look like plurals are actually singular. *News, lens,* and *measles* are all singular nouns.

Objective: Students choose from *has* and *have* or *hasn't* and *haven't* and write the correct verb to agree with the subject of a sentence.

Name _____

Lesson 24

UNIT 2: Usage

Linking Lessons: You might find it helpful to review Lesson 14 on contractions formed with the word *not*.

Subject-Verb Agreement: *Has/Have, Hasn't/Haven't*

Rule
Use **has** or **hasn't** when you talk about one person, place, or thing. *Hasn't* means "has not."

Use **have** or **haven't** when you talk about more than one person, place, or thing and with *you* and *I*.

Example
West Virginia **has** three state songs.
Trevor **hasn't** seen the old mining towns in Colorado.

Have you ever been to the Alamo in Texas?
I **haven't** been paid yet.

Write *has*, *have*, *hasn't*, or *haven't* to complete each sentence.

1. Arkansas ___has___ the only working diamond mine in North America.
2. Kentucky and Ohio ___have___ the Ohio River as a border.
3. Do you ___have___ a map of the United States?
4. Nevada ___has___ the most wild horses.
5. The people of Montana ___have___ Yellowstone National Park in their state.
6. I ___haven't___ seen the cliff dwellings in New Mexico.
7. Mia lives in North Dakota, but she ___hasn't___ been to the Dinosaur Museum.
8. Mississippi ___hasn't___ been part of the United States as long as Vermont has.
9. Hawaii's Mauna Loa volcano ___hasn't___ erupted since 1984.
10. Most of my classmates ___haven't___ been to all five Great Lakes.

Count 1 point for each correct answer.

_____ My Score
10 Top Score

Extension
Write three sentences describing how your bedroom at home is different than your friend's. Use *has/have* and *hasn't/haven't*.

FYI: Some nouns are considered plural even though they refer to a singular thing. For example, the words *goods*, *riches*, *savings*, and *thanks* require plural verbs when used as subjects.

Objective: Students review subject-verb agreement using the verbs *am/is/are*, *was/were*, *isn't/aren't*, *wasn't/weren't*, *doesn't/don't*, *has/have*, and *hasn't/haven't*.

Name _____

Review Lessons 19–24

- Write *am*, *is*, *are*, *was*, or *were* to complete each sentence. Choose from the words in parentheses.

1. Legends __**are**__ stories about heroes. (is, are)

2. Many legends __**were**__ written about King Arthur. (were, was)

- Write *isn't*, *aren't*, *wasn't*, or *weren't* to complete each sentence. Choose from the words in parentheses.

3. A fable __**isn't**__ a true story. (aren't, isn't)

4. "The Cat Who Became a Poet" __**wasn't**__ written about a real cat. (wasn't, weren't)

- Write *doesn't* or *don't* to complete each sentence.

5. A poem __**doesn't**__ have to rhyme.

6. Some poems that __**don't**__ rhyme are written in free verse.

7. A haiku __**doesn't**__ have very many lines.

- Write *has*, *have*, *hasn't*, or *haven't* to complete each sentence. Choose from the words in parentheses.

8. A biography __**has**__ a real person as its subject. (has, have)

9. We __**have**__ a lot of biographies in our library. (have, has)

10. My class __**hasn't**__ finished reading Picasso's biography yet. (haven't, hasn't)

• Lessons 19, 20   • Lessons 21, 22   • Lesson 23   • Lesson 24

Count 1 point for each correct answer.   _____ My Score
10 Top Score

UNIT 2: Usage

Objective: Students choose and write present tense verbs correctly.

Name _____

Lesson 25

UNIT 2: Usage

Linking Lessons: You might find it helpful to review Lesson 5 on verbs and Lessons 19–24 on subject-verb agreement. Lessons 26 and 27 address regular past tense and irregular past tense verbs.

Verbs: Present Tense

Rule	Example
A **present tense** verb tells about an action that happens now.	A panda **eats** bamboo.
A verb changes when there is more than one person or thing doing the action and when it is used with the pronouns *I* and *you*.	Pandas **eat** bamboo. I **eat** bagels.

Write the correct present tense verb in each sentence. Choose from the words in parentheses.

1. Most animals must ___find___ their own food. (find, finds)
2. An animal ___competes___ with other animals for food. (compete, competes)
3. Living things ___need___ energy to survive. (need, needs)
4. Energy ___moves___ through food chains. (move, moves)
5. A food chain ___begins___ with a producer. (begins, begin)
6. Plants ___make___ their own food from the sun's energy. (makes, make)

Write a present tense verb for each subject.   **Answers will vary.**

7. The eagles _____
8. The rain _____
9. The teacher _____
10. The flowers _____

Count 1 point for each correct answer.

_____ My Score
10 Top Score

Extension
Pretend you are at the zoo. Write three sentences about what you see, hear, and smell.

FYI: While many English words can be used as both a noun and a verb (for example, *drink*, *act*, and *fight*), there are few examples of this in other languages.

Objective: Students form and write regular past tense verbs correctly.

Name _____

Lesson 26

UNIT 2: Usage

Linking Lessons: You might find it helpful to review Lesson 5 on verbs. Lesson 27 addresses irregular past tense verbs.

Verbs: Regular Past Tense

Rule	Example
Add -*ed* to form the **past tense** of most verbs.	open–opened paint–painted
For verbs ending in *e*, drop the final *e* before adding -*ed*.	bake–baked, smile–smiled
For verbs ending in a single vowel plus a consonant, double the final consonant before adding -*ed*.	step–stepped, shop–shopped
For verbs ending in *y*, change the final *y* to *i* before adding -*ed*.	cry–cried, marry–married

Write the past tense of the verb in parentheses.

1. The Pilgrims' first winter in Plymouth almost __ruined__ them. (ruin)
2. Many people __died__ from hunger and disease. (die)
3. The governor was __worried__. (worry)
4. The Pilgrims __needed__ help. (need)
5. They __learned__ a lot from Native Americans. (learn)
6. Squanto was the man who __helped__ them the most. (help)
7. With his help, the Pilgrims __raised__ corn. (raise)
8. Squanto __shared__ his knowledge, and the Pilgrims __listened__. (share, listen)
9. He __saved__ the Plymouth colony. (save)

Count 1 point for each correct answer.

_____ My Score
10 Top Score

Extension
Write about something you did last night.

FYI: In Latin, a verb can have as many as 120 inflections. In English, a verb never has more than five forms.

Objective: Students form and write irregular past tense verbs correctly.

Name _____

Lesson 27

UNIT 2: Usage

Linking Lessons: You might find it helpful to review Lesson 5 on verbs. Lesson 26 covers regular past tense verbs.

Verbs: Irregular Past Tense

Rule	Example	
The past tense forms of some verbs do not end in *-ed*. These verbs are called **irregular verbs.**	think–thought bite–bit fall–fell	break–broke win–won tell–told

Write the past tense form of the verb in parentheses.

1. In the early 1900s, many immigrants __came__ to the United States. (come)
2. Most of them __rode__ in boats. (ride)
3. The food they __ate__ on the boats wasn't very good. (eat)
4. Immigrants __brought__ new cultures to America. (bring)
5. They __spoke__ different languages. (speak)
6. Immigrants __had__ many different jobs. (have)
7. Children __sold__ candy and newspapers on the streets. (sell)
8. As the number of immigrants __grew__, they weren't all allowed to stay. (grow)
9. Those who did stay __felt__ very lucky. (feel)
10. Immigrants __made__ this country strong. (make)

Count 1 point for each correct answer.

_____ My Score
10 Top Score

Extension
Find out about your family's heritage. Draw a family tree.

FYI: Encourage students to say the past tense form to decide whether a verb takes *-ed* or is irregular. *Telled* doesn't sound right, but *told* does. Remind students to look up a verb in a dictionary if they aren't sure about its past tense form.

Objective: Students use the correct past tense forms of the verb *come*.

Lesson 28

UNIT 2: Usage

Linking Lessons: Lessons 29–34 address other past tense verb forms using helping verbs.

Verb Forms: Came/Come

Rule

Came is a verb that tells about something that happened in the past. *Came* is always used alone.

Come can also tell about something that happened in the past, but it needs a helper. Use helping words like *have, has,* and *had* with *come*.

Example

Rain finally **came** and ended the dry spell.

The rain **had come** too late to save some of the crops.

Write *came* or *come* in each sentence.

1. Utah's state name __came__ from a Navajo word meaning "higher up."
2. In 1865 the U.S. Civil War had __come__ to an end.
3. Lots of people have __come__ to Florida to visit Walt Disney World.
4. Many slaves __came__ to northern states where they could be free.
5. The American bald eagle __came__ to be a symbol of our country.
6. The mayor has __come__ to our school to give a speech.
7. We saw a rainbow when the sun __came__ out.
8. These eggs __came__ from a free-range farm.
9. The new book about Michael Jordan has finally __come__ in at our library.
10. A tour group has __come__ to the National Cowboy Hall of Fame in Oklahoma.

Count 1 point for each correct answer.

_____ My Score
10 Top Score

Extension
Write about the last time you had relatives at your house.

FYI: Throughout the sixteenth and seventeenth centuries, the verbs *hath* and *doth* evolved into *has* and *does*.

Objective: Students use the correct past tense forms of the verb *see*.

Name _____

Lesson 29

UNIT 2: Usage

Linking Lessons: Lesson 28 and Lessons 30–34 address other past tense verb forms using helping verbs.

Verb Forms: Saw/Seen

Rule
Saw is a verb that tells about something that happened in the past. *Saw* is always used alone.

Seen also tells about something that happened in the past, but it needs a helper. Use helping words like *have, has,* and *had* with *seen*.

Example
I **saw** the chick hatch from its egg.

I **have seen** a lot of animals born on this farm.

Write *saw* or *seen* in each sentence.

1. Abby and Matthew __saw__ a cheetah at the zoo.
2. They have __seen__ the fastest land animal.
3. Abby went to the aquarium and __saw__ the sharks.
4. She has never __seen__ a shark up close.
5. Matthew had already __seen__ the sharks.
6. He went to the aviary instead and __saw__ tropical birds.
7. The zoo guide asked Matthew if he has ever __seen__ a toucan before.
8. Matthew __saw__ the toucan's bright feathers and long bill.
9. Abby __saw__ Matthew go in the reptile house.
10. They looked at lizards and talked about what they had __seen__ .

Count 1 point for each correct answer.

_____ My Score

10 Top Score

Extension
Write three sentences about the last time you and your friends went to a farm, park, or zoo. What did you see?

FYI: Shakespeare often used nouns as verbs, as adverbs, and as adjectives.

Objective Students use the correct past tense forms of the verb *do*.

Name _____

Lesson 30

UNIT 2: Usage

Linking Lessons: Lessons 28, 29, and 30–34 address other past tense verb forms using helping verbs.

Verb Forms: Did/Done

Rule
Did is a verb that tells about something that happened in the past. *Did* is always used alone.

Done also tells about something that happened in the past, but it needs a helper. Use helping words like *have, has,* and *had* with *done*.

Example
Sylvie **did** yoga to help her relax.

Her teacher **has done** yoga for ten years.

Write *did* or *done* in each sentence.

1. __Did__ you know the horned toad is actually a lizard?
2. Acid rain has __done__ damage to our environment.
3. Dian Fossey __did__ research with gorillas.
4. How many times __did__ Bjorn Borg win at Wimbledon?
5. Red Cross volunteers have __done__ a lot to help people.
6. What had Ronald Reagan __done__ before he became president?
7. Picasso __did__ most of his artwork in France.
8. Alejandro has __done__ seven of the ten decathlon events.
9. Have you __done__ your book report on *Make Way for Ducklings*?
10. The architect __did__ a sketch before he made the final drawing.

Count 1 point for each correct answer.

_____ My Score
10 Top Score

Extension
Write three sentences telling about something you did yesterday.

FYI: English is the most studied language in the world. Some English words that have become almost universal are *airport, telephone, O.K.,* and *jeans*.

37

Objective: Students review present tense verbs, regular past tense verbs, irregular past tense verbs, and the verb forms *came/come*, *saw/seen*, and *did/done*.

Name _____

Review Lessons 25–30

- **Write the correct present tense verb in each sentence. Choose from the words in parentheses.**

1. Our bodies __need__ different vitamins. (need, needs)
2. Vitamin A __helps__ our bones and eyes. (helps, help)

- **Write the past tense form of the verb in parentheses.**

3. Computers __changed__ the way we work and live. (change)
4. I __copied__ the report to a floppy disk. (copy)
5. If you __saved__ your document, you can see it again later. (save)
6. Charles Lindbergh __flew__ from New York to Paris in 33 1/2 hours. (fly)
7. Harriet Ziefert __wrote__ the book *A New Coat for Anna*. (write)

- **Write the correct verb in each sentence. Choose from the words in parentheses.**

8. Martin Luther King, Jr., __came__ to Washington, D.C. (come, came)
9. I had __seen__ other Aztec ruins in New Mexico. (seen, saw)
10. Scientists have __done__ a lot to improve public health. (did, done)

• Lesson 25
• Lessons 26, 27
• Lessons 28–30

Count 1 point for each correct answer.

_____ My Score
10 Top Score

UNIT 2: Usage

Objective: Students use the correct past tense forms of the verb *go*.

Name _____

Lesson 31

UNIT 2: Usage

Linking Lessons: Lessons 28–30 and Lessons 32–34 address other past tense verb forms using helping verbs.

Verb Forms: Went/Gone

Rule
Went is a verb that tells about something that happened in the past. *Went* is always used alone.

Gone also tells about something that happened in the past, but it needs a helper. Use helping words like *have*, *has*, and *had* with *gone*.

Example
The price of cars **went** down.

The prices **had gone** down because of assembly lines.

Write *went* or *gone* in each sentence.

1. Our class ___went___ to a car factory on a field trip.
2. We had ___gone___ to find out how an assembly line works.
3. The car ___went___ along a conveyor belt.
4. The body was painted after it had ___gone___ through the welding stations.
5. The wheels, engine, seats, and other parts ___went___ in next.
6. After the car has ___gone___ through the line, it is carefully checked.
7. People make sure the car wasn't scratched as it ___went___ down the line.
8. Cars from this factory have ___gone___ to dealers who sell them.
9. We could have ___gone___ to another factory to see an assembly line.
10. I'm glad we ___went___ to this one.

Count 1 point for each correct answer.

_____ My Score
10 Top Score

Extension
Tell about a trip you have taken. Use complete sentences to tell about your trip.

FYI: In the Korean language, one must choose from six verb suffixes in accordance with the social status of the person being addressed.

Objective: Students use the correct past tense forms of the verb *run*.

Lesson 32

Name _____

UNIT 2: Usage

Linking Lessons: Lessons 28–31 and Lessons 33–34 address other past tense verb forms using helping verbs.

Verb Forms: *Ran/Run*

Rule	Example
Ran is a verb that tells about something that happened in the past. *Ran* is always used alone.	A lion **ran** toward the herd of zebras.
Run can also tell about something that happened in the past, but it needs a helper. Use helping words like *have*, *has*, and *had* with *run*.	The zebras **have run** away from the lion.

Write *ran* or *run* in each sentence.

1. Many people have __run__ in the Boston Marathon.
2. We __ran__ an ad in the newspaper for our garage sale.
3. The baby had __run__ a fever with her ear infection.
4. Bob Dole __ran__ for president in 1996.
5. This battery has __run__ out of energy.
6. Carl Lewis __ran__ in many Olympic events.
7. The car stopped when it __ran__ out of gas.
8. A ferryboat has __run__ between the two islands for years.
9. The colors in my painting have __run__ together.
10. The musical Cats __ran__ on Broadway for many years.

Extension
Write directions on how to play a recess game. Be sure to tell things in the right order.

Count 1 point for each correct answer.

_____ My Score
10 Top Score

FYI: In German, the verb *ride* has 16 forms. It only has five forms in English (*ride, rides, riding, rode,* and *ridden*).

Objective: Students use the correct past tense forms of the verb *eat*.

Lesson 33

UNIT 2: Usage

Linking Lessons: Lessons 28–32 and Lesson 34 address other past tense verb forms using helping verbs.

Verb Forms: Ate/Eaten

Rule

Ate is a verb that tells about something that happened in the past. *Ate* is always used alone.

Eaten also tells about something that happened in the past, but it needs a helper. Use helping words like *have*, *has*, and *had* with *eaten*.

Example

The panda **ate** bamboo stems.

The panda **has eaten** 45 pounds of bamboo today.

Write *ate* or *eaten* in each sentence.

1. Mateo would feel better if he had __eaten__ breakfast.
2. Keiko and I __ate__ fresh pineapple in Hawaii.
3. The astronauts have __eaten__ their freeze-dried food.
4. Jessie needed protein, so she __ate__ an egg.
5. The pretzels I __ate__ made me thirsty.
6. The cat is overweight because it has __eaten__ too much.
7. Kyle has __eaten__ four servings of fruit today.
8. We __ate__ corned beef and cabbage on St. Patrick's Day.
9. Have you ever __eaten__ with chopsticks?
10. The horse __ate__ some hay.

Count 1 point for each correct answer.

_____ My Score
10 Top Score

Extension
Write about what each person in your family had for breakfast this morning.

FYI: The grammatical forms of verbs include number, person, and tense.

Objective: Students use the correct past tense forms of the verb *give*.

Lesson 34

UNIT 2: Usage

Linking Lessons: Lessons 28–33 address other past tense verb forms using helping verbs.

Verb Forms: Gave/Given

Rule
Gave is a verb that tells about something that happened in the past. Gave is always used alone.

Given also tells about something that happened in the past, but it needs a helper. Use helping words like *have*, *has*, and *had* with *given*.

Example
France **gave** the Statue of Liberty to the United States.

Has the United States **given** gifts to other countries?

Write *gave* or *given* in each sentence.

1. Many soldiers have __given__ their lives for their country.
2. Dr. Chen __gave__ me a flu shot.
3. My family has __given__ money to the Humane Society and other charities.
4. Voyager 2 __gave__ us close-up pictures of Uranus's moons.
5. The manager __gave__ the job to Nathan.
6. Fossils have __given__ us a better idea of what dinosaurs were like.
7. Natalie found her ring when she had __given__ up looking for it.
8. Abraham Lincoln __gave__ a famous speech at Gettysburg.
9. Noise from the airport has __given__ me a headache.
10. The Nineteenth Amendment __gave__ women the right to vote.

Count 1 point for each correct answer.

_____ My Score
10 Top Score

Extension
Write about a favorite gift you have given or received.

FYI: The literacy rate in Vatican City is 100%.

Objective: Students avoid using double negatives.

Lesson 35

Name _____

UNIT 2: Usage

Linking Lessons: It might be helpful to review Lesson 14 on contractions formed with *not*. Lessons 21–24 address subject-verb agreement using various contractions formed with *not*.

Double Negatives

Rule
Sometimes negative words like *no, none, nothing, never,* and *no one* are used in a sentence. The word *not* and contractions made with *not* are also negative words.

Only one negative word should be used in a sentence.

Example
You should **never** look directly at the sun.

Don't forget to wash your hands before eating.

Incorrect
There **wasn't no one** at the gym.

Correct
There **was no one** at the gym.

Choose the correct word to complete each sentence.

1. There aren't ___**any**___ ski slopes in Florida. (any, no)
2. Baby insects don't look ___**anything**___ like their parents. (anything, nothing)
3. Bamboo isn't ___**a**___ tree. (no, a)
4. People ___**can**___ never tell the twins apart. (can, can't)
5. No one has ___**ever**___ found two identical snowflakes. (ever, never)
6. A purebred dog ___**is**___ no better pet than a mutt. (isn't, is)
7. The dentist said I don't have ___**any**___ cavities. (no, any)
8. You ___**should**___ never ride your bike without a helmet. (should, shouldn't)
9. I've never read ___**anything**___ like the book *Stevie*. (nothing, anything)
10. George Washington didn't ___**ever**___ live in the White House. (ever, never)

Count 1 point for each correct answer.

_____ My Score
10 Top Score

Extension
Write three sentences with negative words like *no, never, nothing,* and contractions formed with the word *not.*

FYI: A double negative isn't necessarily wrong; however, it creates a positive meaning. Using a double negative is wrong if a sentence is supposed to have a negative meaning.

Objective: Students form and use comparative and superlative adjectives correctly.

Lesson 36

UNIT 2: Usage

Name _____

Linking Lessons: You might find it helpful to review Lesson 6 on adjectives.

Adjectives: Comparing

Rule	Example
To **compare two nouns,** add *-er* to most adjectives. Use *more* plus the adjective for most adjectives with two or more syllables.	The lemonade is **sweeter** than the lemon. The lemonade is **more delicious** than the lemon.
To **compare more than two nouns,** add *-est* to most adjectives. Use *most* plus the adjective for most adjectives with two or more syllables.	This is the **ripest** banana in the bunch. This is the **most perfect** banana in the bunch.

Circle the correct adjective in each sentence.

1. The chef made her   **more special** (**most special**)   dessert for us.
2. A coconut shell is (**harder**) **hardest**   than a peanut shell.
3. I used the   **bigger** (**biggest**), **hotter** (**hottest**)   peppers I could find.
4. This red potato is (**more tender**) **most tender**   than that yellow one.
5. Cherry tomatoes are (**smaller**) **smallest**   than plum tomatoes.

Write the correct form of the adjective in parentheses.

6. This chowder is the ___most flavorful___ soup I've eaten. (flavorful)
7. Pancakes are ___flatter___ than waffles. (flat)
8. Frozen vegetables are ___fresher___ than canned ones. (fresh)
9. Is a pie ___more difficult___ to make than a cake? (difficult)

Count 1 point for each correct answer.   _____ My Score   10 Top Score

Extension
Write down your favorite recipe to share with the class.

FYI: Tell students that for adjectives ending in *e*, drop the final *e* before adding the ending. For adjectives ending in a single vowel plus a consonant, double the final consonant. For adjectives ending in a single vowel plus *y*, change the *y* to *i*.

Objective: Students review the verb forms *went/gone*, *ran/run*, *ate/eaten*, and *gave/given*. They will also review double negatives and comparative and superlative adjectives.

Name _____

Review Lessons 31–36

- Write the correct verb form in each sentence. Choose from the words in parentheses.

1. John Glenn has __gone__ into space twice. (went, gone)
2. The first time he __went__ was in 1962. (went, gone)
3. The president of the school board __ran__ the meeting. (ran, run)
4. She said we had __run__ out of money for new books. (ran, run)
5. I haven't __eaten__ at the new Italian restaurant. (ate, eaten)
6. Mariah said she __ate__ some good pasta there. (ate, eaten)
7. Emily Post __gave__ people tips on good manners. (gave, given)
8. Her book has __given__ us good advice for many years. (gave, given)

- Circle the correct word to complete each sentence.

9. Astrology isn't nothing (anything) like astronomy.
10. Secret agents cannot talk to (anyone) no one about their work.
11. A circle doesn't have (any) no corners.

- Write the correct adjective to complete each sentence.

12. The sun is the __biggest__ thing in the solar system. (big)
13. Venus has a __rockier__ surface than Earth. (rocky)
14. Pluto is the __most distant__ planet from the sun. (distant)
15. Mercury is the __closest__ planet to the sun. (close)

•Lessons 31–34
•Lesson 35
•Lesson 36

Count 1 point for each correct answer.

_____ My Score
15 Top Score

UNIT 2: Usage

45

Objective: Students review cumulatively Unit 1 (Grammar) and Unit 2 (Usage).

Name _____

Cumulative Review — Units 1–2

- **Unit 1** — Circle the nouns and underline the verbs in the sentence below.

   1. Acid (rain) can <u>fall</u> many (miles) from the (factories) that <u>cause</u> it.

- **Unit 1** — Write the plural possessive form of each noun.

   2. sandwich __sandwiches'__   3. buggy __buggies'__

- **Unit 1** — Circle the pronouns and underline the adjectives in the sentences below.

   4. A <u>female</u> kangaroo carries (her) baby in a pouch.

- **Unit 1** — Circle the complete subject and underline the complete predicate in each sentence.

   5. (The bones in your head) <u>make up your skull</u>.

- **Unit 1** — Write a sentence with the words below. Use the correct end mark. Answers will vary.

   6. a new bicycle _____

- **Unit 2** — Write a, an, or the in each sentence.

   7. Soil is __a__ resource we depend on.

   8. __The__ roots of trees hold soil in place.

- **Unit 2** — Make a contraction using the words in parentheses.

   9. Maya Angelou's childhood __wasn't__ happy. (was, not)

   10. That __didn't__ stop her from becoming a famous writer. (did, not)

- **Unit 2** — Write the correct pronoun in each sentence. Use the words in parentheses.

   11. Tiger Woods became a pro golfer when __he__ was only 20. (him, he)

   12. I hope Tiger will pose for a picture with Ming and __me__. (I, me)

UNIT 2: Usage

Name _____

Cumulative Review

- Unit 2 **Write the correct verb in each sentence. Use the words in parentheses.**

    13. The curtain will close when the play has __come__ to an end. (came, come)

    14. A long-distance runner __tries__ to break away from the pack. (tries, try)

    15. The first woman in space __wasn't__ American. (wasn't, weren't)

    16. A geyser __doesn't__ spout cold water. (doesn't, don't)

    17. Legos __were__ created in the 1930s. (was, were)

    18. We should have __gone__ to see the King Tut exhibit. (went, gone)

- Unit 2 **Write the past tense form of each verb.**

    19. wear __wore__   20. rot __rotted__

- Unit 2 **Circle the word that belongs in each sentence.**

    21. A maiden dog hasn't (**ever**) never had any puppies.

    22. You should never put (**anything**) nothing sharp in your ear.

- Unit 2 **Write the correct form of the adjective in parentheses.**

    23. A year on Mars is __longer__ than a year on Earth. (long)

    24. The spine-tailed swift is the world's __fastest__ bird. (fast)

Count 1 point for each correct answer.   _____ My Score
30 Top Score

UNIT 2: Usage

Objective: Students are assessed on their knowledge of usage.

Name _____

UNIT 2 Inventory

Write a, an, or the in each sentence.
Lesson 13

1. Ireland is __an__ island.
2. __The__ capital of Ireland is Dublin.

Write a contraction to complete each sentence. Use the words in parentheses.
Lesson 14

3. Some people __don't__ think zoos are a good idea. (do, not)
4. They feel animals __shouldn't__ be in cages. (should, not)

Circle the correct pronoun in each sentence.
Lessons 15–18

5. Sam and me (**I**) are learning about the Anasazi people.
6. The Anasazi boiled yucca leaves, then peeled (**them**) it.
7. They used the yucca leaves to make his (**their**) sandals.

Write the correct verb to complete each sentence.
Lessons 19–24

8. Glass mirrors __were__ used in Italy in 1300. (was, were)
9. A mirror __doesn't__ have to be flat. (doesn't, don't)
10. Sometimes mirrors __are__ curved. (is, are)

Write the correct past tense verb to complete each sentence.
Lessons 26–27

11. Horses __pulled__ the covered wagons. (pull)

12. It __took__ a long time to get from Missouri to Oregon. (take)

Write the correct verb to complete each sentence.
Lessons 28–34

13. Many people had __gone__ to California in the 1840s. (went, gone)
14. They __ran__ to San Francisco looking for gold. (ran, run)
15. Not many people __saw__ big pieces of gold. (saw, seen)
16. The Gold Rush had __given__ new life to San Francisco. (gave, given)

Write the correct word to complete each sentence.
Lesson 35

17. Some babies don't have __any__ hair when they are born. (no, any)
18. You __should__ never look at the sun with binoculars. (shouldn't, should)

Circle the correct adjective in each sentence.
Lesson 36

19. Uranus has the more unusual (**most unusual**) orbit of all the planets.
20. A tree kangaroo's tail is (**longer**) longest than its body.

Count 1 point for each correct answer.

_____ My Score

20 Top Score

UNIT 3
Mechanics

Objective: Students use a capital letter to begin a sentence.

Name _____

Before starting this unit, you may wish to give the Inventory on page 72 as a diagnostic test.

Lesson 37

Linking Lessons: You might find it helpful to review Lesson 8 on recognizing sentences.

Capitalization: The Beginning of a Sentence

Rule	Example
A **sentence** always begins with a capital letter.	**P**eople visit zoos to learn about animals. **D**oesn't the Cleveland Zoo have a rain forest exhibit?

Circle the beginning letter of each sentence if it should be a capital letter.

(t)he San Diego Wildlife Park is in California. (g)iraffes and other animals roam free at this park. (w)hat kinds of birds are at the park? (t)here are flamingos and storks. (y)ou can see animals from all over the world. (t)he park has five different habitats. (c)an people get close to the animals? (v)isitors ride through the park on a train.

Write two sentences about what is happening in the picture.

1. Answers will vary. Check students' sentences to be sure they begin with a capital letter and end with an end mark.

2. _____

Count 1 point for each correct answer.

_____ My Score
10 Top Score

Extension
Write three sentences about an animal that interests you.

FYI: Expressions used as sentences are also capitalized. For example: No way! Why not? Oh, well.

49

Objective: Students distinguish common nouns from proper nouns and correctly capitalize proper nouns.

Name _____

Lesson 38

UNIT 3: Mechanics

Linking Lessons: You might find it helpful to review Lesson 1 on nouns. Lessons 37 and 39–45 address other rules for capitalization. Lessons 47–50 and 52 address capitalization and punctuation.

Capitalization: Common and Proper Nouns

Rule	Example
A **common noun** names any person, place, or thing. Common nouns do not begin with a capital letter.	A **woman** designed the **memorial**.
A **proper noun** names a particular person, place, or thing. Proper nouns begin with a capital letter.	**Maya Ying Lin** designed the **Vietnam Veterans Memorial**.

Circle each letter that should be a capital letter.

1. Philadelphia is one of the (u)nited (s)tates' most historic cities.
2. It was founded by (w)illiam (p)enn.
3. There were 13 colonies in (a)merica in the early 1700s.
4. The largest city in the colonies was (p)hiladelphia.
5. Philadelphia was the first capital of (p)ennsylvania.
6. The capital was moved from (p)hiladelphia to (l)ancaster in 1799.
7. The (d)elaware (r)iver runs by the city.

Write a proper noun for each common noun. Answers will vary.

8. my teacher _____
9. an ocean _____
10. the president _____
11. the street _____

Count 1 point for each correct answer.

_____ My Score

15 Top Score

Extension
Write a paragraph about someone you know in another city.

FYI: Explain to students that most adjectives derived from proper nouns are also capitalized (France–French, Shakespeare–Shakespearean).

Objective: Students capitalize the names of persons and pets.

Lesson 39

UNIT 3: Mechanics

Linking Lessons: You might find it helpful to review Lesson 38 on common and proper nouns.

Capitalization: Persons and Pets

Rule
The name of a **person** or a **pet** begins with a capital letter.

Example
Melanie's dog **Lucky** followed her home one day.

Circle each letter that should be a capital letter.

1. Do (h)olly and her sister (a)llison have pets?
2. Is (t)rixie the name of (h)olly's dog?
3. I think (t)rixie is the white dog.
4. We heard (a)llison's puppy, (g)unther, barking.
5. The girls' dad, (b)rian, walks the dogs.
6. Sometimes (b)rian takes the cat, (b)ert, along.
7. Does their other cat, (e)rnie, go with them?
8. No, (e)rnie is afraid of (m)adison, who lives next door.
9. Isn't (m)adison the neighbors' pig?
10. Her parents gave (h)olly a turtle.
11. The turtle, (s)igmund, lives in a fish tank.
12. Do (h)olly and (a)llison have any other pets?
13. They have two rabbits named (h)oney and (p)umpkin.

Count 1 point for each correct answer.

_____ **My Score**
20 Top Score

Extension
Make a list of pets you have had or have known. Write the type of pet beside each name.

FYI: An individual's preference for spelling and capitalization of his or her name should always be respected. For example, the poet e. e. cummings did not capitalize his name.

Objective: Students capitalize the word *I*.

Name _____

Lesson 40

UNIT 3: Mechanics

Linking Lessons: You might find it helpful to review Lesson 18 on using *I* and *me*. Lessons 37–39 and 41–45 address other rules for capitalization. Lessons 47–50 and 52 address capitalization and punctuation.

Capitalization: The Word *I*

Rule	Example
The word *I* is always written as a capital letter.	Marco and I are science partners.

Write the word *I* in each sentence.

1. Marco and __I__ are studying forms of energy.
2. __I__ wanted to do an experiment with light.
3. The teacher said __I__ could if Marco agreed.
4. Marco said he thought __I__ had a good idea.
5. First, __I__ planted some seeds in two cups.
6. __I__ put one cup by the window and one in the closet.
7. Every day, Marco and __I__ checked the seeds.
8. The seeds that got sunlight grew faster, as __I__ predicted.

Write two sentences using the word *I*. Answers will vary.

9. _____

_____

10. _____

_____

Count 1 point for each correct answer.

_____ **My Score**

10 Top Score

Extension
Write a few sentences describing what you look like today.

FYI: Some trademarks, such as *aspirin*, *nylon*, and *fax*, have become established as common nouns and are no longer capitalized. Check a current dictionary if you're unsure of a trademark's status.

Objective: Students correctly capitalize words that indicate family relationships.

UNIT 3: Mechanics

Linking Lessons: Lessons 37–40 and 42–45 address other rules for capitalization. Lessons 47–50 and 52 address capitalization and punctuation.

Capitalization: Relatives

Rule
Names that show how you are **related** to someone begin with a capital letter if they are used in place of or as part of the relative's name.

Words that name relatives do not begin with a capital if they follow *my, our, your, his, her,* or *their.*

Example
I flew to Sacramento to visit **A**unt Savon and **U**ncle Michael.

I flew to Sacramento to visit my **a**unt and **u**ncle.

Circle each letter that should be a capital letter.

1. Emilio and Sonia went to see ⓖrandma Lina.
2. They hadn't seen their grandma for a long time.
3. Sonia gave ⓐunt Ana and ⓤncle Roberto a hug.
4. Emilio asked his aunt and uncle to come to ⓖrandma Lina's house.
5. Grandma Lina had invited all of their cousins.
6. Sonia couldn't wait to see ⓒousin Luisa's new baby.
7. "We should call ⓜom and ⓓad," said ⓒousin Luisa.
8. She told them, "We're here with ⓖrandma, Ana, and Roberto."

Write a sentence about a special family celebration. Use a relative's name.
Answers will vary.
9. _____

Count 1 point for each correct answer.

_____ My Score
10 Top Score

Extension
Write a paragraph or short story about one of your relatives.

FYI: In some cases, the word that describes a relationship is capitalized even when it follows a possessive. Look at the following sentence: *Jenny took us to dinner with her Aunt Janel. Aunt* is capitalized in this case because Jenny thinks of her as *Aunt Janel,* and the two words form a unit.

Objective: Students capitalize the names of the months of the year.

Name _____

Lesson 42

UNIT 3: Mechanics

Linking Lessons: Lessons 37–41 and 43–45 address other rules for capitalization. Lessons 47–50 and 52 address capitalization and punctuation.

Capitalization: Months

Rule	Example
The names of the **months** of the year begin with a capital letter.	We're having a fall harvest party in **O**ctober.

January	April	July	October
February	May	August	November
March	June	September	December

Write the name of the month that belongs in each sentence.

1. New Year's Day is the first of __January__.

2. Presidents' Day comes in __February__.

3. Our St. Patrick's Day party is __March__ 17.

4. Independence Day is the fourth day of __July__.

5. The last full month of summer is __August__.

6. My family goes to the pumpkin farm in __October__.

7. We celebrate Thanksgiving in __November__.

8. The last day of the year is in __December__.

9. My birthday is in __Answers will vary.__

10. School ends in __Answers will vary.__

Count 1 point for each correct answer.

_____ **My Score**
10 Top Score

Extension
Write three sentences about your favorite season. Use the names of months in your sentences.

FYI: Explain to students that the names of seasons (*winter, spring, summer,* and *fall* or *autumn*) are not capitalized.

Objective: Students review capitalization of the first word of a sentence, proper nouns, names of persons and pets, the word *I*, relatives, and months.

Name _____

Review Lessons 37–42

- **Write two sentences about the weather.** Answers will vary.
  1. _____
  2. _____

- **Circle each letter that should be a capital letter.**
  3. Roy (r)ogers was a famous (a)merican cowboy.
  4. Roy's family moved from (o)hio to (c)alifornia when he was young.
  5. Didn't (r)oy and his wife, (d)ale (e)vans, have a television show?
  6. I saw a picture of Dale's horse, (b)uttermilk.

- **Write the word *I* in each sentence.**
  7. The doctor asked me how __I__ felt.
  8. She said __I__ had a fever.

- **Circle each letter that should be a capital letter.**
  9. Mom and (d)ad took us on vacation in (j)uly.
  10. We went to see (g)randpa Pete.
  11. My sister and I had fun at (a)unt Laura's house.
  12. She invited us to stay with her and (u)ncle Larry until (a)ugust.
  13. I wanted to stay with my aunt.
  14. Mom and (d)ad said we couldn't stay.
  15. We had too much to do before school started in (s)eptember.

Lesson 37 •Lessons 38–39 •Lesson 40 •Lessons 41–42

Count 1 point for each correct answer.

_____ **My Score**
20 Top Score

UNIT 3: Mechanics

Objective: Students capitalize the names of the days of the week.

Name _____

Lesson 43

UNIT 3: Mechanics

Linking Lessons: Lessons 37–42, 44, and 45 address other rules for capitalization. Lessons 47–50 and 52 address capitalization and punctuation.

Capitalization: Days of the Week

| **Rule** | **Example** |
| The names of the **days of the week** begin with a capital letter. | I'm going to the dentist on **Tuesday**. |

Write the name of the day of the week that belongs in each sentence.

Sunday	Wednesday	Friday
Monday	Thursday	Saturday
Tuesday		

1. The first day of the week is ___Sunday___.
2. The day after Tuesday is ___Wednesday___.
3. The day before Wednesday is ___Tuesday___.
4. The day after Thursday is ___Friday___.
5. The day before Friday is ___Thursday___.
6. The day after Sunday is ___Monday___.
7. The day before Sunday is ___Saturday___.
8. Yesterday was ___Answers will vary.___
9. Today is ___Answers will vary.___
10. Tomorrow is ___Answers will vary.___

Count 1 point for each correct answer.

_____ My Score
10 Top Score

Extension
Make a planner for next week. Beneath each day of the week, write something you plan to do on that day.

FYI: The Julian calendar, developed in 45 B.C., established the months of the year and days of the week.

Objective Students capitalize the names of holidays.

Name _____

Lesson 44

UNIT 3: Mechanics

Linking Lessons: Lessons 37–43 and 45 address other rules for capitalization. Lessons 47–50 and 52 address capitalization and punctuation.

Capitalization: Holidays

Rule	Example
Each word in the name of a holiday or special day begins with a capital letter.	We celebrate Independence Day in July.

Circle each letter that should be a capital letter.

1. George Washington and Abraham Lincoln's birthdays are celebrated on (p)residents' (d)ay.

2. December 26 is the first day of (k)wanzaa.

3. The first (e)arth (d)ay celebration was on April 22, 1970.

4. Veterans of United States wars are honored on (v)eterans (d)ay.

5. Cards, flowers, and candy are popular (v)alentine's (d)ay gifts.

6. My friend Debra always tricks me on (a)pril (f)ool's (d)ay.

7. An Act of Congress in 1949 made June 14 (f)lag (d)ay.

8. We don't have school on (l)abor (d)ay.

9. Don't forget to wear green on (s)t. (p)atrick's (d)ay.

10. Many people like to watch the parades on (t)hanksgiving (d)ay.

11. I cook my parents breakfast on (m)other's (d)ay and (f)ather's (d)ay.

Count 1 point for each correct answer.

_____ **My Score**

25 Top Score

Extension
Write three sentences about your favorite holiday.

FYI: The word *holiday* came from Old English words that mean *holy day*.

57

Objective: Students correctly capitalize the names of places.

Lesson 45

UNIT 3: Mechanics

Linking Lessons: You may wish to review Lesson 38 on common and proper nouns. Lessons 37, 39–44, 47–50, and 52 address other rules for capitalization and punctuation.

Capitalization: Places

Rule	Example
The names of places such as countries, states, cities, towns, streets, lakes, rivers, parks, and schools begin with capital letters.	The **W**hite **H**ouse is at 1600 **P**ennsylvania **A**venue. Professor Sakai teaches at **S**tanford **U**niversity in **C**alifornia.

Circle the names of places with capital letters in the sentences below.

1. Is (m)ount (r)ainier the tallest mountain in (w)ashington?
2. About 20,000 workers created (c)entral (p)ark.
3. Jenny went to the (w)ellington (s)chool on (r)eed (r)oad.
4. Ferries run between the islands in (l)ake (e)rie.
5. The biggest wheat-growing states are (n)orth (d)akota and (k)ansas.
6. The capital of (n)ew (j)ersey is (t)renton, but the largest city is (n)ewark.
7. The busiest port in the (u)nited (s)tates is in (l)ouisiana.
8. The (c)olorado (r)iver runs through the (g)rand (c)anyon.

Count 1 point for each correct answer.

_____ My Score
25 Top Score

Extension
Write directions from your school to your house.

FYI: The word *city* should be capitalized only when it is part of the official name of a city (Salt Lake City) or part of a nickname (City of Angels).

Objective: Students correctly use commas in the names of places.

Name _____

Lesson 46

UNIT 3: Mechanics

Linking Lessons: You might find it helpful to review Lesson 45 on capitalizing the names of places. Lesson 50 addresses capitalization and punctuation of addresses.

Punctuation: Commas in Place Names

Rule	Example
A comma is used between the name of a city and the state or country that follows it.	The Louvre is a museum in Paris, France.
A comma also follows the name of the state or country if it isn't the last word in the sentence.	Sydney, Australia, was the site of the 2000 Olympics.

Write commas where they belong in the following sentences.

1. The world's first alphabet was found in Ugarit, Syria.

2. Varanasi, India, is one of the oldest cities in the world.

3. Cape Canaveral, Florida, is where NASA launches its space shuttles.

4. The first known coins were made in Lydia, Turkey.

5. The Inuit artist Kenojuak lived in Cape Dorset, Canada.

6. Kobe, Japan, was shaken by an earthquake in 1995.

7. Dakar, Senegal, is West Africa's most important port.

8. What do you think people eat for breakfast in Two Egg, Florida?

9. Frankfurt, Germany, hosts a large book fair every October.

10. The Nobel Peace Prize is given in Oslo, Norway.

Count 1 point for each correct answer.

_____ My Score

15 Top Score

Extension
Make a list of ten state capitals. Then write a sentence using two of them.

FYI: Omitting the second comma that sets the name of a state or country apart from the rest of the sentence is a common mistake. Remind students to check for this. Example: *Demitrius was born in Detroit*, Michigan, *in 1992.*

59

Objective: Students use correct capitalization and punctuation for book and story titles.

Lesson 47

UNIT 3: Mechanics

Name _____

Linking Lessons: Lessons 37–44 address various rules for capitalization. Lessons 48–50 and 52 address other rules for capitalization and punctuation.

Capitalization and Punctuation:
Book and Story Titles

Rule	Example
The first word in the **title of a book** or **story** begins with a capital letter. Begin other words in a title with a capital letter except articles and prepositions.	Harriet Ziefert wrote the book *A New Coat for Anna*.
	a, an, the, and, but, for, of, to, with, under, by, at, in
When writing with a computer, use italics for the title.	Shel Silverstein wrote *A Light in the Attic*.
When you handwrite the title of a book, underline it.	*A New Coat for Anna was illustrated by Anita Lobel.* (cursive, underlined)
Quotation marks are used around the **titles of stories**.	Our class is reading the story "The Blind Men and the Elephant."

Write each title with correct capital letters and punctuation.
Count one point for each correctly capitalized letter and punctuation.

1. I enjoyed reading Margaret Mahy's story the cat who became a poet.
   "The Cat Who Became a Poet"

2. Diane Hoyt-Goldsmith wrote the book carving the pole.
   Carving the Pole

3. the keeping quilt is my favorite book by Patricia Polacco.
   The Keeping Quilt

4. a tale of the brothers grimm is a story by Terry Fertig.
   "A Tale of the Brothers Grimm"

Count 1 point for each correct answer.

_____ My Score
20 Top Score

Extension
Make a list of your five favorite books or stories.

FYI: While the title of a book is italicized, quotation marks should be used around titles that denote only part of a book, such as titles of chapters, lessons, or sections.

Objective: Students correctly capitalize personal titles.

Name _____

Lesson 48

UNIT 3: Mechanics

Linking Lessons: Lessons 37–44 address various rules for capitalization. Lessons 47, 49, 50, and 52 address other rules for capitalization and punctuation.

Capitalization and Punctuation: Titles

Rule	Example
Titles of respect begin with a capital letter.	My art teacher is **M**iss Lowe.
If a title is abbreviated, it begins with a capital letter and ends with a period.	I asked **Dr.** Wick if I had any cavities.

Circle each letter that should be a capital letter. Put a period after each title that is an abbreviation.

1. Ask (m)s. Velazquez if she is ready for lunch.
2. The first American woman to graduate from medical school was (d)r. Elizabeth Blackwell.
3. (m)r. and (m)rs. woods are proud of their son.
4. Did you ever see the horse named (m)r. Ed?
5. Ling met (m)iss Sato at the park.
6. Some people call the president of the United States "(m)r. President."
7. We took our dog to (d)r. hill for her check-up.
8. Have you read *From the Mixed-Up Files of* (m)rs. Basil E. Frankweiler?
9. "The Belle of Amherst" was a nickname given to (m)iss Emily Dickinson.
10. I think (m)s. Washington is the best soccer coach.

Count 1 point for each correct answer.

_____ My Score

20 Top Score

Extension
Write the name of a friend, a relative, and a doctor. Include a title with each name.

FYI: Job titles are usually not capitalized when they are used alone (for example, the *judge from Ohio* as opposed to *Judge Malone*).

61

Objective: Students review capitalization of days of the week, holidays, and places. They also review capitalization and punctuation of book and story titles and personal titles.

Name _____

Review Lessons 43–48

- Write the days of the week in order from first to last.

1. Sunday
2. Monday
3. Tuesday
4. Wednesday
5. Thursday
6. Friday
7. Saturday

- Circle the letters that should be capital letters.

8. We planted some spruce trees in honor of (a)rbor (d)ay.

9. May 30 is (m)emorial (d)ay.

- Circle the letters that should be capital letters. Write commas where they belong.

10. The (C)olville (r)iver runs from (B)rooks (r)ange, (A)laska, to the (B)eaufort (s)ea.

11. How many students go to (n)orthwestern (u)niversity in (E)vanston, (I)llinois?

- Write each title with correct capital letters and punctuation.

12. the bremen town musicians is a story by the Brothers Grimm.
    "The Bremen Town Musicians"   (6 points total)

- Circle the letters that should be capital letters. Write periods where they belong.

13. Go, Dog. Go! was my favorite (d)r. Seuss book.

14. I also liked his book (m)r. Brown Can Moo! Can You?

• Lesson 43
• Lesson 44
• Lessons 45–46
• Lesson 47
• Lesson 48

Count 1 point for each correct answer.

_____ My Score
35 Top Score

62   UNIT 3: Mechanics

Objective: Students correctly capitalize and punctuate abbreviations and titles.

Lesson 49

UNIT 3: Mechanics

Linking Lessons: You might find it helpful to review Lesson 48 on capitalization and punctuation of personal titles. Lessons 47, 50, and 52 address other rules for capitalization and punctuation.

Capitalization and Punctuation:
Abbreviations and Initials

An **abbreviation** is a shortened form of a word. **Initials** can be used as an abbreviation.

Rule	Example	
Abbreviations for the days of the week, months of the year, titles, and places begin with a capital letter and end with a period.	Sunday—**Sun.** Monday—**Mon.** Friday—**Fri.** January—**Jan.** April—**Apr.** August—**Aug.** September—**Sept.**	December—**Dec.** Mister—**Mr.** Mistress—**Mrs.** Street—**St.** Road—**Rd.** Avenue—**Ave.**
Capital letters are used for initials. Put a period after each letter.	The address for the Baseball Hall of Fame is **P.O.** Box 590, Cooperstown, NY 13326.	

Circle the letters that should be capital letters. Write in periods where they belong.

1. The ABC television network is at 77 West 66th (s)t. in New York City.

2. The third (m)on. in (f)eb. is when we celebrate Presidents' Day.

3. The author of *Stuart Little* is (e).(b). White.

4. National Grandparents' Day is (s)ept. 10.

5. (d)r. Mary (e). Walker was the only woman to receive the Medal of Honor.

6. (d)r. and (m)rs. King were civil rights leaders.

Count 1 point for each correct answer.

_____ **My Score**
20 Top Score

Extension
Write the names of three people you know. Use a title and the first and middle initials.

FYI: Some shortened forms of words are not abbreviations and don't require a period. *Exam, limo, temp,* and *deli* are some examples.

Objective: Students use correct capitalization and punctuation in addresses.

Name _____

Lesson 50

UNIT 3: Mechanics

Linking Lessons: Lessons 47–49 and 51–52 address other rules for capitalization and punctuation.

Capitalization and Punctuation: Addresses

Rule	Example
A capital letter is used for the first word in every line of an address. Capital letters are also used throughout an address except for words like *and, of,* and *the.* Abbreviations are used for people's titles, names of streets or roads, and state names in addresses. A comma is used between the city and state. Periods aren't used in the postal abbreviations for state names.	Ms. Karen Hall and Mr. Ken Hall 5150 Rosecrans Ave. Hawthorne, CA 90205

Circle the letters that should be capitalized and insert the proper punctuation.

1. mr. ronald mcDonald
   1 mcDonald Plaza
   oak brook, il 60521

2. american girl magazine
   8400 fairway pl.
   middletown, wi 53562

3. students and youth against racism
   p.o. box 1819
   madison square station
   new york, NY 10159

Count 1 point for each correct answer.

_____ **My Score**
35 Top Score

Extension
Write the address of your school. Write your name on the first line, and use a title.

FYI: The zip code was instituted in 1963. The U.S. Postal Service began using the expanded nine-digit zip code in 1983 to increase the efficiency of mail sorting and delivery.

Objective: Students use correct punctuation in dates and times.

Name _____

Lesson 51

UNIT 3: Mechanics

Linking Lessons: Lessons 46, 53, and 54 address other rules for punctuation. Lessons 47–50 and 52 cover rules for capitalization and punctuation.

Punctuation: Dates and Time

Rule
When writing a **date,** use a comma before and after the year if it is written with the month and the day.

Don't use a comma if only the month and the year are given.

When writing a **time,** use the abbreviations a.m. (before noon) and p.m. (after noon).

Example
On July 31, 1976, Nadia Comaneci scored the first perfect "10" in gymnastics.

In July 1976 a Romanian gymnast scored the first perfect "10."

At 5:09 p.m. their baby girl was born.

Insert the correct punctuation or cross out unnecessary punctuation.

1. Jamal had to cancel his 10:00 a.m. meeting.

2. On July 18, 1955, Disneyland opened in California.

3. In May, 1973 the U.S. space station *Skylab* was launched.

4. We're going to be late for the 7:20 p.m. movie.

5. In November, 1987 a talking watch was introduced in Japan.

6. Kecia's haircut was changed from 9:15 a.m. to 2:45 p.m.

7. On November 18, 1928, Mickey Mouse became a movie star.

8. The wedding will be at 6:30 p.m. on October 12, 2002.

9. In September, 1960 Wilma Rudolph won three Olympic gold medals.

10. Who is the pilot for the 11:00 a.m. flight to London?

Count 1 point for each correct answer.

_____ **My Score**
20 Top Score

Extension
Make up a schedule of your classes and appointments for tomorrow.

FYI: Lowercase letters are not always used for *a.m.* and *p.m.* However, that is the style students should follow for the lessons in this book.

Objective: Students use correct capitalization and punctuation in the parts of a friendly letter.

Lesson 52

UNIT 3: Mechanics

Linking Lessons: You might find it helpful to review Lessons 44, 49, 50, and 51 on capitalization and punctuation of titles, abbreviations and initials, addresses, and dates and times.

Capitalization and Punctuation: Letters

Rule	Example
The **heading** of a friendly letter has your address and the date.	301 N. Water St. Wilmington, NC 28412 July 24, 2001
The **greeting** usually begins with the word *Dear*. After that, you write the name of the person who will get the letter. Write a comma after the name.	Dear Chika,
The **body** of the letter is where you write your message.	I am writing to you from our hotel. We are having a wonderful vacation!
The **closing** is where you end the letter. Capitalize only the first word. Use a comma after the closing, then sign your name.	Yours truly, *Miki*

Circle the letters that should be capital letters. Add punctuation.

702 Harper (s)t.
Sioux Falls, SD 57105
January 5, 2001

(d)ear Emma,

   I am so excited! Today my parents told me that we are going to visit you in New York this summer. We'll be there Aug. 1–5. Will you go with me to look at the Statue of Liberty?

(y)our friend,
Brad

Count 1 point for each correct answer.

_____ My Score
10 Top Score

Extension
Write a letter to a friend or relative. Tell about one of your hobbies.

FYI: In 1909 it cost two cents to send a one-ounce letter in the United States.

Objective: Students use commas correctly in a series of items.

Name _____

Lesson 53

UNIT 3: Mechanics

Linking Lessons: Lessons 46, 51, and 54 cover other rules for punctuation. Lessons 47–50 and 52 address capitalization and punctuation.

Punctuation: Commas in a Series

Rule	Example
A comma is used after each item in a **series** except the last one.	Jorge is bringing cheese, bread, grapes, and water to the picnic.

Write commas where they belong in each sentence.

1. Red, yellow, and blue are the primary colors.
2. I saw an ear, nose, and throat doctor when I lost my voice.
3. Is it a cougar, lion, tiger, or panther?
4. Baseball players need a glove, bat, batting helmet, and cleats.
5. Pulleys, planes, and levers are all simple machines.
6. The chef put red onions, celery, carrots, and peppers in the salad.
7. Some people are allergic to things like dust, pollen, feathers, and pet hair.
8. Jessica has brown hair, blue eyes, and braces.
9. Mail carriers deliver letters in rain, sleet, hail, or snow.
10. Marta collects stamps, coins, and hats.

Count 1 point for each correct answer.

_____ My Score

25 Top Score

Extension
Write three sentences about your favorite foods, animals, and activities. List at least three items in each sentence.

FYI: If *and, or,* or *nor* is used between the items in a series, commas are not necessary. For example, *I don't know if I'll buy a red car or black car or white car.*

Objective: Students use correct punctuation when writing quotations.

Lesson 54

UNIT 3: Mechanics

Linking Lessons: Lessons 46, 51, and 53 cover other rules for punctuation. Lessons 47–50 and 52 address capitalization and punctuation.

Punctuation: Quotations

Rule	Example
Quotation marks are used right before and right after a speaker's words. A quotation begins with a capital letter.	Patrick Henry declared, "Give me liberty or give me death!"
Use a comma to separate a quotation from the rest of the sentence. Put an end mark inside the closing quotation mark at the end of the sentence.	"I must have no hatred or bitterness towards anyone," said Edith Cavell. Chief Joseph said, "I will fight no more forever."

Write commas and quotation marks where they belong in each sentence. Circle letters that should be capital letters.

1. Davy Crocket said, "(B)e sure you are right, then go ahead."

2. "(Y)ou're either part of the solution or part of the problem," stated Eldridge Cleaver.

3. Oprah Winfrey said, "(I) still have my feet on the ground, I just wear better shoes."

4. "(H)ome is not where you live but where they understand you," said Christian Morgenstern.

5. Duke Ellington said, "(A) problem is a chance for you to do your best."

Count 1 point for each correct answer.

_____ **My Score**
20 Top Score

Extension
Write three sentences telling what you heard people say today. Use quotation marks around their exact words.

FYI: You might want to explain to students the use of commas to separate the speaker from his or her quotation.

Objective: Students review capitalization and punctuation used in abbreviations and initials, addresses, and letters. They also review punctuation of dates and times, series of items, and quotations.

Name _____

Review Lessons 49–54

- **Circle the letters that should be capital letters. Write in commas and periods where they belong.**

1. The fourth (t)hurs. in (n)ov. is Thanksgiving.
2. I loved (j.r.r.) Tolkien's book *The Hobbit*.
3. Kei is meeting (m)s. (h)an at 2:00 p.m. tomorrow.
4. On July 6, 1957, Althea Gibson won at Wimbledon.

- **Write the address with correct capitalization and punctuation.**

5. winners on wheels   Winners on Wheels
   2842 business park ave   2842 Business Park Ave.
   fresno ca 93727   Fresno, CA 93727

- **Circle the letters that should be capital letters. Write commas where they belong.**

6. (d)ear Bryant,
7. (s)incerely yours,

- **Write commas where they belong in each sentence.**

8. Asia, Africa, and Europe are three of the seven continents.
9. Do you want a muffin, donut, or bagel?
10. Pine, cedar, and redwood trees have cones.

- **Write commas and quotation marks where they belong in each sentence. Circle letters that should be capital letters.**

11. Charles Lamb said, "(a) sweet child is the sweetest thing in nature."
12. "(T)he Eagle has landed," stated Neil Armstrong.

Count 1 point for each correct answer.

_____ My Score

45 Top Score

UNIT 3: Mechanics

Objective: Students review cumulatively Unit 1 (Grammar), Unit 2 (Usage), and Unit 3 (Mechanics).

Name _____

Cumulative Review — Units 1–3

- **Unit 1** — Circle the nouns and underline the verbs below.
    1. A (frog) blinks and swallows at the same (time).

- **Unit 1** — Write the plural form of each noun.
    2. lily __lilies__   3. sinus __sinuses__

- **Unit 1** — Circle the pronouns and underline the adjectives below.
    4. The green lizard lifted (its) tiny feet off the hot sand.

- **Unit 1** — Circle the complete subject and underline the complete predicate.
    5. (Both hands and feet) are used to play the drums.
    6. (The bass drum) makes a deep sound.

- **Unit 1** — Find where each sentence begins and ends. Circle letters that should be capital letters. Write periods where they are needed.

    People need water to live. (T)hey have found ways to collect it and store it. (D)ams are built to help people control their water supply.

- **Unit 2** — Make a contraction using the words in parentheses.
    7. Lions __don't__ purr. (do, not)
    8. The prairie dog __isn't__ really a dog. (is, not)

- **Unit 2** — Write the correct pronoun in each sentence. Use the words in parentheses.
    9. The gymnast lifted __his__ arms to grab the rings. (him, his)
    10. __She__ and her husband are dentists. (She, Her)

- **Unit 2** — Choose the correct verb for each sentence.
    11. Peta has __given__ me her book *The Little Prince*. (gave, given)
    12. A helicopter __doesn't__ look like an airplane. (doesn't, don't)

UNIT 3: Mechanics

Name _____

Cumulative Review

• Unit 2 **Choose the correct word in the sentence.**

13. Don't let ___any___ light shine on your film. (no, any)

• Unit 3 **Circle the letters that should be capital letters.**

Dakar is the capital of (S)enegal, a country in (A)frica. (D)akar's population changes during the year. From (N)ovember to (J)une many farmers go to the city to work. (T)hey go back to their farms during the rainy season. (A)unt Serena and (U)ncle (K)evin are going to (S)enegal next (F)riday. (I) asked my aunt to send me a picture of the (A)tlantic (O)cean.

• Unit 3 **Write the title with correct capital letters and punctuation.**

14. The story the country mouse and the city mouse is a fable.
    "The Country Mouse and the City Mouse"

• Unit 3 **Circle the letters that should be capital letters. Write in periods and commas where they belong.**

15. The Hockey Hall of Fame is on (Y)onge (S)t. in Toronto, Canada.
16. (P)(D). Eastman wrote some of the (D)r. (S)euss books.

• Unit 3 **Circle the letters that should be capital letters. Write commas and quotation marks where they belong.**

17. Charlie Brown said," (G)ood grief!"
18. The cold-hearted queen said," (L)et them eat cake."

Count 1 point for each correct answer.   _____ My Score
                                          65 Top Score

UNIT 3: Mechanics

Objective: Students are assessed on their knowledge of mechanics.

Name _____

UNIT 3 Inventory

Circle the letters that should be capital letters.
Lessons 37–45

1. ⓜartin Ⓒrane's dog is named Ⓔddie.
2. Ⓐre you going to see Ⓒrater Ⓛake when you're in Ⓞregon?
3. Mother's Ⓓay is on the second Ⓢunday in Ⓜay.
4. The Ⓐrctic Ⓞcean is the smallest of the four oceans.

Write in commas where they belong.
Lessons 46, 53

5. Los Angeles, California, is often covered in smog.
6. Spheres, cubes, and pyramids are solid figures.

Write each title with correct capital letters and punctuation.
Lesson 47

7. Michele M. Surat wrote the book angel child, dragon child.
   <u>Angel Child, Dragon Child</u>

Circle each letter that should be a capital letter. Write in periods and commas where they belong.
Lessons 48, 49, 51

8. On Ⓜay 29, 1953, Ⓜr. Ⓔ. Ⓗillary and Ⓜr. Ⓣ. Ⓝorgay reached the top of Mt. Everest.

Write the address with correct capital letters and punctuation.
Lesson 50

children's digest
1100 waterway blvd
p o box 567
indianapolis in 46202

<u>Children's Digest</u>
<u>1100 Waterway Blvd.</u>
<u>P. O. Box 567</u>
<u>Indianapolis, IN 46202</u>

Circle the letters that should be capital letters. Write commas where they belong.
Lesson 52

9. Ⓓear Ⓜayor Ⓣruman,
10. Ⓨours truly,

Circle the letters that should be capital letters. Write commas and quotation marks where they belong.
Lesson 54

11. Queen Victoria said, "Ⓦe are not amused."
12. "We're not in Kansas anymore," said Dorothy.

Count 1 point for each correct answer.

_____ My Score
60 Top Score

UNIT 4

Vocabulary

Objective: Students use context clues to define words.

Name _____

Lesson 55

Linking Lessons: Lesson 56 provides practice with using context clues to choose the appropriate definition of multiple-meaning words.

Word Meaning from Context

Before starting this unit, you may wish to give the Inventory on page 82 as a diagnostic test.

Rule
Sometimes you can figure out the meaning of a word by looking at how it is used in a sentence. The other parts of a sentence that help you define a word are called **context clues.**

Example
We had to **classify** the stones by size and color.

Size and **color** are context clues. Stones could be sorted into different groups by their size and color. *Classify* means "sort."

Circle the letter that tells the best meaning of the bold word in each sentence. Underline the context clues.

1. The Declaration of Independence and the Constitution are important **documents** in our country's history.
   - **(a)** written statements that give information
   - b. new books

2. Hundreds of people **bustled** down the busy street.
   - a. relaxed
   - **(b)** walked quickly

3. The Washington Monument is a famous **structure** in Washington, D.C.
   - **(a)** something that is built
   - b. a body of water

4. The Supreme Court is made up of a **panel** of nine judges.
   - **(a)** group
   - b. law

5. The best way to settle an argument is to **compromise.**
   - **(a)** give and take
   - b. fight harder

Count 1 point for each correct answer.

_____ My Score
10 Top Score

Extension
Start a personal dictionary. When you come across a new word, write it in your dictionary with a definition and an example sentence.

FYI: The word *tell* once meant "to count." That meaning is no longer used, but the term *bank teller* is a remnant from it.

73

Objective: Students choose the appropriate definition for multiple-meaning words in context.

Name _____

Lesson 56

UNIT 4: Vocabulary

Linking Lessons: You might find it helpful to review Lesson 55 on defining words from context.

Multiple-Meaning Words

Rule
Many words have **more than one meaning.** Use context clues to figure out the correct meaning.

The word *banks* can mean "businesses that hold, lend, and exchange money" or "grounds that border a body of water." The word *River* tells you that the second definition of *banks* is the correct meaning.

Example
Our nation's capital is on the **banks** of the Potomac River.

Circle the letter that tells the meaning of the bold word in each sentence.

1. The English setter had a **litter** of ten puppies.
    - (a.) baby animals born at one birth
    - b. rubbish; trash

2. Maria gets a **kick** out of watching scary movies.
    - a. to hit with the foot
    - (b.) an exciting feeling; thrill

3. A pitcher throws more than the **rest** of the baseball players.
    - a. peace; relaxation
    - (b.) those that remain; others

4. Thomas Edison had a **hunch** his lightbulb would work.
    - (a.) a guess or feeling
    - b. to bend or stoop

5. We have to **charge** the battery in our telephone.
    - a. to run toward in an attack
    - (b.) to fill with energy

Count 1 point for each correct answer.

_____ My Score
5 Top Score

Extension
Make a list of three words that have more than one meaning. Write at least two definitions for each word.

FYI: The word *fine* fills two pages in the *Oxford English Dictionary*. It has fourteen definitions as an adjective, six as a noun, and two as an adverb.

Objective: Students identify and write synonyms.

Name _____

Lesson 57

UNIT 4: Vocabulary

Linking Lessons: Lesson 58 addresses antonyms.

Synonyms

Rule	Example
Words that have the same or almost the same meaning are called **synonyms.**	An **adult's** heart beats about 70 times a minute. A **grown-up's** heart beats about 70 times a minute.

Choose a word from the box that means almost the same thing as one of the numbered words. Write the synonym on the line beside the numbered word.

pretty	scared	author	difficult	cloudy
cart	calm	dangerous	steps	box

1. carton __box__
2. wagon __cart__
3. unsafe __dangerous__
4. lovely __pretty__
5. peaceful __calm__

6. writer __author__
7. hard __difficult__
8. stairs __steps__
9. gloomy __cloudy__
10. afraid __scared__

Write a synonym for each word below. **Answers will vary.**

11. happy _____
12. angry _____
13. grin _____

14. cold _____
15. large _____

Count 1 point for each correct answer.

_____ My Score
15 Top Score

Extension
Choose one of the words from this page and write at least two more synonyms for it.

FYI: The people of the Trobriand Islands of Papua New Guinea have about a hundred words for yams.

Objective: Students identify and write antonyms.

Name _____

Lesson 58

UNIT 4: Vocabulary

Linking Lessons: Lesson 57 addresses synonyms.

Antonyms

> **Rule**
> Words that have opposite meanings are called **antonyms**.
>
> **Example**
> The **largest** ocean on Earth is the Pacific Ocean.
>
> The **smallest** ocean on Earth is the Arctic Ocean.

Choose a word from the box that has the opposite meaning of one of the numbered words. Write the antonym on the line beside the numbered word.

| high | past | quickly | first | perfect |
| short | smooth | night | open | late |

1. early ___late___
2. tall ___short___
3. day ___night___
4. low ___high___
5. rough ___smooth___

6. slowly ___quickly___
7. last ___first___
8. closed ___open___
9. damaged ___perfect___
10. future ___past___

Write an antonym for each word below. Answers will vary.

11. light _____
12. quiet _____
13. hard _____

14. new _____
15. top _____

Count 1 point for each correct answer.

_____ My Score
15 Top Score

Extension
Choose two words from this page and write another antonym for each one.

FYI: Sometimes the same word has opposite meanings. For example, *cleave* can mean "split apart" or "stick together."

76

Objective: Students use the homophones *to*, *too*, and *two* correctly.

Name _____

Lesson 59

UNIT 4: Vocabulary

Linking Lessons: Lesson 60 covers the homophones *there*, *their*, and *they're*.

Homophones—To, Too, Two

Homophones are words that sound the same but are spelled differently and have different meanings.

Rule	Example
To means "toward."	Oxygen we breathe in goes **to** our lungs.
Too means "also" or "more than enough."	The director Spike Lee writes and acts **too**.
Two is the number between one and three.	Twins are **two** babies born at one birth.

Write *to*, *too*, or *two* in each sentence.

1. An angle is made of __two__ lines or rays.
2. Earth leans __to__ one side.
3. Lime and olive are __two__ shades of green.
4. Some flowers won't grow where it's __too__ shady.
5. The *Apollo 13* astronauts returned __to__ Earth in April 1970.
6. The Newbery Medal is given __to__ outstanding authors of children's books.
7. Is the hole in the ozone layer getting __too__ big?
8. Ballet and tap are __two__ kinds of dance.
9. Chess is my favorite game, but I like checkers __too__.
10. If you go __to__ Philadelphia, you can see the Liberty Bell.

Count 1 point for each correct answer.

_____ My Score
10 Top Score

Extension
Make a list of other homophones.

FYI: Many terms cause confusion in our language. For example, *all right* should be spelled as two words. The spelling *alright* is not generally considered correct.

77

Objective: Students use the homophones *there, their,* and *they're* correctly.

Name _____

Lesson 60

UNIT 4: Vocabulary

Linking Lessons: Lesson 59 covers the homophones *to, too,* and *two.*

Homophones—There, Their, They're

Homophones are words that sound the same but are spelled differently and have different meanings.

Rule	Example
There means "at or in that place."	Many actors live in New York because of the theaters **there.**
Their means "belonging to them."	Snakes don't chew **their** food.
They're means "they are."	Don't pick the tomatoes until **they're** red.

Write *there, their,* or *they're* in each sentence.

1. Many people take __*their*__ vacations at national parks.
2. __*They're*__ in states all across the country.
3. At Biscayne in Florida __*there*__ are islands with coral reefs.
4. The rock formations at Bryce Canyon have been __*there*__ for centuries.
5. Caribou, moose, and sheep make __*their*__ home at Denali.
6. __*There*__ are Native American cliff dwellings at Zion.
7. __*They're*__ more than 1,000 years old.
8. Some people go to Hot Springs for __*their*__ health.
9. Visitors like the springs because __*they're*__ warm.
10. At Big Bend __*there*__ are dinosaur fossils.

Extension
Write three sentences using the homophones *do, due,* and *dew.*

Count 1 point for each correct answer.

_____ My Score
10 Top Score

FYI: Point out to students the differences in meaning between the terms *everyday* (an adjective meaning "common or ordinary") and *every day* (an adjective and a noun meaning "each day").

Objective: Students review defining words in context, multiple-meaning words, synonyms, antonyms, and homophones.

Name _____

Review Lessons 55–60

- **Circle the letter that tells the best meaning of the bold word. Use context clues to figure out the meaning.**

   1. Some beetles have **ferocious** horns for fighting.
      - (a.) fierce; violent
      - b. long and thin

   2. A frog can move fast enough to catch a **fly**.
      - a. to move through the air
      - (b.) an insect

- **Write a synonym on the line beside the word.**   Answers will vary.

   3. glow ____shine____   4. plane ____jet____

- **Write an antonym on the line beside the word.**

   5. straight ____curly____   6. dirty ____clean____

- **Write *to*, *too*, or *two* in the sentences below.**

   7. ____Two____ members of city council missed the town meeting.

   8. The mayor was absent ____too____.

- **Write *there*, *their*, or *they're* in the sentences below.**

   9. ____There____ are some bees that live in hives.

   10. Most bees live on ____their____ own.

• Lesson 55 • Lesson 56 • Lesson 57 • Lesson 58 • Lesson 59 • Lesson 60

Count 1 point for each correct answer.

_____ My Score
10 Top Score

UNIT 4: Vocabulary

Objective: Students review cumulatively Unit 1 (Grammar), Unit 2 (Usage), Unit 3 (Mechanics), and Unit 4 (Vocabulary).

Name _____

Cumulative Review — Units 1–4

- Unit 1

    Circle the nouns and underline the verbs in the following sentences. Add the correct end mark to each sentence.

    1. What (chimp) flew into (space) ?
    2. The (United States) sent (Ham) into (space) .

- Unit 1

    Find where each sentence begins and ends. Circle letters that should be capital letters. Write in periods where they are needed.

    Toads and frogs are related. (T)hey look alike, but they are not the same. Toads have bumpy skin. (F)rogs have smooth skin. (F)rogs are better jumpers than toads.

- Unit 2

    Write the correct pronoun in each sentence. Use the words in parentheses.

    3. Lian and __I__ learned about habitats. (me, I)
    4. Polar bears eat seals and fish in __their__ natural habitat. (their, they)
    5. An animal also uses nonliving things in __its__ habitat. (its, their)

- Unit 2

    Circle the correct verb in each sentence.

    The Great Plains (stretch) stretches from Mexico to Canada. The explorer Zebulon Pike had (gone) went to this area. He seen (saw) endless fields of grass. Native Americans had came (come) there to live thousands of years before Pike arrived.

- Unit 2

    Write the correct word from the parentheses.

    6. Don't let __any__ light shine on your film. (any, no)
    7. A photo is __more exact__ than a drawing. (more exact, most exact)

- Unit 3

    Circle the letters that should be capital letters. Write in commas and periods where they belong.

    8. When it is 12:00 p.m. in (n)ew (y)ork, it is 7:00 a.m. in (h)onolulu, (h)awaii.

Name _____

Cumulative Review

9. Every (T)uesday my uncle works at (R)iverside (H)ospital with (A)unt (B)eth and Mr. Takamura.

10. Rubber, gum, waxes, and dyes can be made from rain forest trees.

11. (M)ore people live in (T)okyo, (J)apan, than in any other Japanese city.

• Unit 3 **Circle the letters that should be capital letters. Write in the correct punctuation for each sentence.**

12. (T)he soccer players yelled, "(O)ne, two, three . . . let's go!"

13. (I) wonder who wrote the story "(T)he (F)ive (C)hinese (B)rothers."

• Unit 4 **Circle the letter that tells the meaning of the bold word in the sentence.**

14. Maple trees lose their leaves in the **fall**.
    a. to drop or tumble   (b). autumn

• Unit 4 **Write a synonym and an antonym for each word.** Answers will vary.

15. sad   synonym: _____   antonym: _____

16. quiet   synonym: _____   antonym: _____

• Unit 4 **Write *to*, *too*, or *two* in each sentence.**

17. Have you had __two__ servings of milk today?

18. Don't eat foods that have __too__ much fat.

• Unit 4 **Write *there*, *their*, or *they're* in each sentence.**

19. Some elements get __their__ names from the scientists who discovered them.

20. __There__ are more than 100 kinds of elements

21. __They're__ all listed in the Periodic Table.

Count 1 point for each correct answer.   _____ My Score
                                                 70 Top Score

UNIT 4: Vocabulary

Objective: Students are assessed on their knowledge of vocabulary.

Name _____

UNIT 4 Inventory

Circle the letter that tells the best meaning of the bold word in each sentence. Use context clues. Lesson 55

1. The **employer** gave her workers the day off.
   a. a nurse
   (b.) a person who hires and pays others to work

2. Some lobsters travel as a group when they **migrate** to deeper water.
   (a.) move from one place to another
   b. hunt for food

Circle the letter that tells the meaning of the bold word. Lesson 56

3. This shiny pebble will look nice in my **rock** collection.
   (a.) a piece of stone
   b. a kind of popular music

4. The doctor put a **cast** on Mai Lin's broken arm.
   a. a group of actors
   (b.) a stiff mold

Write the synonym on the line beside the numbered word. Lesson 57

damp   sofa   lamp

5. couch _____sofa_____
6. wet _____damp_____
7. light _____lamp_____

Write the antonym on the line beside the numbered word. Lesson 58

fresh   dull   north

8. shiny _____dull_____
9. rotten _____fresh_____
10. south _____north_____

Write *to*, *too*, or *two* in each sentence.

11. I went ___to___ buy gloves for my ski trip.

12. Baseball players wear gloves ___too___ .

Write *there*, *their*, or *they're* in each sentence.

13. I collect four-leaf clovers, but ___they're___ hard to find.

14. In a rain forest ___there___ are many layers of trees.

15. Wildflowers grow on ___their___ own.

Count 1 point for each correct answer.

_____ My Score
15 Top Score

UNIT 5

Reference Skills

Objective: Students identify letters of the alphabet in order and organize words in alphabetical order.

Name _____

Lesson 61

Linking Lessons: Lessons 62 and 63 address using a dictionary and other reference sources that are organized in alphabetical order.

Alphabetical Order

Before starting this unit, you may wish to give the Inventory on page 92 as a diagnostic test.

Rule
When a list of words follows the order of the letters in the alphabet, the list is in **alphabetical order.** If the first two letters of a word are the same, look at the second letter to put words in alphabetical order.

Example
Aardema, Verna

Cameron, Ann

Clifton, Lucille

Write *before* or *after* in each blank.

1. s comes __before__ v
2. e comes __after__ b
3. o comes __before__ q
4. k comes __before__ m
5. x comes __before__ y

Write the list of words in alphabetical order on the lines below.

nose   neck   arm
ankle   back

6. _____ankle_____
7. _____arm_____
8. _____back_____
9. _____neck_____
10. _____nose_____

Count 1 point for each correct answer.

_____ My Score
10 Top Score

Extension
Write the names of five classmates in alphabetical order.

FYI: The Chinese language uses characters called radicals instead of an alphabet. The word *song* is formed by combining the radicals for *mouth* and *bird*.

Objective: Students use a dictionary to find the correct spelling, pronunciation, and meaning of words.

Name _____

Lesson 62

UNIT 5: Reference Skills

Linking Lessons: You might find it helpful to review Lesson 61 on alphabetical order.

Using a Dictionary

Rule	Example
A **dictionary entry** shows a word, its syllables, how to say it, and its meanings.	**doc•tor** (dok t´ər) *n.* 1. a person who practices medicine 2. a person who holds the highest university degree
Guide words show the first and last words found on the page.	*Dad* and *dust* could be guide words on the page where you would find the word **doctor**.

Use the dictionary entries to answer the questions.

1. How many syllables does the word *slippery* have? __three__

2. Which word could be found on a page with the guide words *eye* and *flap*? __fizzle__

3. Which meaning of the word *quarter* best fits the following sentence? *We like to go to the shops in the French quarter.* __3__

4. What does the word *angry* mean?
   __mad; annoyed; upset__

5. Which word could be found on a page with the guide words *fleece* and *freckle*? __flit__

---

an•gry (ang´grē) *adj.* mad; annoyed; upset

fiz•zle (fiz´əl) 1. *v.* to make a hissing sound 2. to end weakly after a good start

flit (flit) *v.* to fly lightly and rapidly

quar•ter (kwôr tər) *n.* 1. one of four equal parts; one fourth 2. a coin equal to 25 cents. 3. a part of a city or town

slip•per•y (slip´ərē) *adj.* 1. likely to slip or slide 2. tricky

Pronunciation Guide
at, āpe, mé, it, fôrk, sông, ə = a in *about*, o in *lemon*, u in *circus*

Count 1 point for each correct answer.

_____ **My Score**
5 Top Score

Extension
Look in a dictionary. Write the guide words for *blanket*, *picnic,* and *umbrella.*

FYI: Explain to students that guide words help them find the word they are looking for quickly. Guide words are printed at the top of each page. Words are listed in alphabetical order.

Objective: Students identify the correct reference source to use for finding various kinds of information.

Name _____

Lesson 63

UNIT 5: Reference Skills

Linking Lessons: Lesson 62 provides practice using a dictionary. Lessons 64 and 66 address using a table of contents and an index and reading a map.

Reference Sources

Rule
Books that we can look in to find information are called **reference sources.** Different types of reference books have different kinds of information.

Example
An **atlas** is a collection of maps.

A **dictionary** has information about words.

An **encyclopedia** has general information about many different subjects.

Magazines and **newspapers** give us information about current events.

atlas	dictionary	newspaper
cookbook	encyclopedia	telephone book

Answer the following questions. Choose from the list of reference sources.

1. Which source would tell you how to break the word *community* into syllables? __dictionary__

2. Which source would tell you how to get from your town to another town? __atlas__

3. Which source would tell you about a sale at a store in your town? __newspaper__

4. Which source would tell you about fossils? __encyclopedia__

5. Which source would tell you the name, address, and phone number of the library in your town? __telephone book__

Count 1 point for each correct answer.

_____ My Score
5 Top Score

Extension
Look up the word *potato* in a cookbook, a dictionary, and an encyclopedia. Which source gives you the most information?

FYI: Explain to students that reference materials are available in many forms. Interviews, museums, the Internet, and audiovisual materials are other sources of information.

85

Objective: Students use a table of contents and an index to locate information.

Name _____

Lesson 64

UNIT 5: Reference Skills

Linking Lessons: You might find it helpful to review Lesson 61 on alphabetical order and Lesson 63 on reference sources.

Using a Table of Contents and an Index

A **table of contents** and an **index** are parts of a book that help readers quickly find information.

A **table of contents** lists the sections of a book along with their page numbers. The table of contents is at the front of a book.

An **index** lists the names, places, and topics in a book and shows the page numbers where information can be found. An index is at the back of a book.

ENERGY
Table of Contents

Chapter
1 Forms of Energy   1
2 How Energy Changes Form 23
3 How People Use Energy   45

Index

batteries, 37
heat, 3, 24–30, 47
light, 5, 26–32, 47
natural resources, 18–21
stored energy, 2, 22

Use the table of contents and index to answer the questions.

1. Which chapter would tell you how to measure changes in energy? __Chapter 2__

2. Which pages tell you about stored energy? __pages 2, 22__

3. Which pages would tell you about coal as a natural resource? __pages 18–21__

4. Which chapter would tell you about how people heat their homes? __Chapter 3__

5. Which chapter would tell you how chemical energy becomes electrical energy? __Chapter 2__

Count 1 point for each correct answer.

_____ My Score

5 Top Score

Extension
Think of another index entry to add to the sample index about energy.

FYI: The first edition of *The World Almanac* was published in 1868. When Joseph Pulitzer began publishing it annually in 1886, his goal was to make the almanac a "compendium of universal knowledge."

Objective: Students organize information in an outline.

Name _____

Lesson 65

UNIT 5: Reference Skills

Linking Lessons: Lesson 63 covers reference sources.

Outlines

Rule
An **outline** includes main topics, subtopics, and details. All of the subtopics and details should tell about the main topic.

Example
Colors would be a main topic for the subtopics **red, yellow,** and **blue.**

Read the paragraph. Then choose words or phrases from the box to complete the outline.

Deserts are the driest places in the world. Even though it doesn't rain much in a desert, some kinds of plants and animals can live there. Cacti are desert plants that store the water they need in their stems. The mesquite plant has long roots that find water far under the ground. Camels can live as long as ten days in the desert without water. Their bodies turn fat from their humps into water. Kangaroo rats never drink water. Their bodies make water from the dry seeds they eat.

I. Plant life
   A. Cacti
   B. _Mesquite plants_

II. _Animal life_
   A. _Camels_
      1. Can go 10 days without drinking water
      2. Bodies turn fat into water
   B. _Kangaroo rats_
      1. Never drink water
      2. _Bodies make water from seeds_

| Animal life |
| Bodies make water from seeds |
| Camels |
| Kangaroo rats |
| Mesquite plants |

Count 1 point for each correct answer.

_____ My Score

5 Top Score

Extension
Make an outline of things in the classroom. You might use *people, furniture,* and *pictures* as *main topics.*

FYI: Explain that an outline is a way to organize information about a subject. Point out to students that roman numerals are used for main topics, capital letters for subtopics, and Arabic numerals for details. There should be at least two items under each main topic or subtopic.

Objective: Students use a map as a source of information.

Name _____

Lesson 66

UNIT 5: Reference Skills

Linking Lessons: Lesson 63 covers reference sources, including atlases.

Reading a Map

Rule
The **map key** explains what symbols mean.

A **compass rose** shows which direction is north, south, east, and west. The letters N, S, E, and W are sometimes used as abbreviations.

Example
A tree could be used to show where a park is on a map.

Use the map to answer the following questions.

Tree City

Map Key
- (H) Hospital
- Grocery Store
- Library
- Gas Station

1. Does Main St. run north and south or east and west? __north and south__

2. Which road only goes north off Oak St.? __Birch St.__

3. What building is at the corner of Walnut St. and Maple Dr.? __library__

4. Which direction would you go on Birch St. to get to the hospital? __south__

5. Which roads would you take to get from the hospital to the gas station?
   __Oak St. to Main St.__

Count 1 point for each correct answer.

_____ My Score
5 Top Score

Extension
Make up your own map key with at least three symbols. You can use colors in your symbols.

FYI: Humans made maps even before they developed a system for writing. The oldest known map is a Babylonian clay tablet that dates from about 2500 B.C.

Objective: Students review reference skills including alphabetical order, using a dictionary, choosing reference sources, using a table of contents and an index, making outlines, and reading a map.

Name _____

Review Lessons 61–66

- **Write the following words in alphabetical order.**

    ball   puzzle   piano   bicycle

    ball, bicycle, piano, puzzle

- **Use the dictionary entry to answer the questions.**

    fa • vor (fā´ vər) 1. *n.* an act of kindness 2. *v.* to approve of; to like

    1. How many syllables does the word *favor* have? __two__

    2. Which meaning of *favor* best fits the following sentence? *Carly favors pants instead of dresses.* __number 2__

- **Circle the letter of the correct answer.**

    3. Which of these would tell you how long to bake a chocolate cake?

        a. encyclopedia   b. calendar   c. telephone book   (d). cookbook

    4. Which of these is a main topic that includes the other three words?

        a. baseball   (b). sport   c. hockey   d. bowling

- **Use the table of contents to answer the questions.**

    5. Which chapter would tell you about watercolor paints? __Chapter 3__

    6. Which chapter would tell you how to store a stamp collection? __Chapter 1__

HOBBIES	
Chapter	Page
1 Collecting Things	1
2 Hiking	17
3 Painting	25

• Lesson 61
• Lesson 62
• Lessons 63, 65
• Lesson 64

Count 1 point for each correct answer.

_____ My Score

10 Top Score

UNIT 5: Reference Skills

Objective: Students review cumulatively Unit 1 (Grammar), Unit 2 (Usage), Unit 3 (Mechanics), Unit 4 (Vocabulary), and Unit 5 (Reference Skills).

Name _____

Cumulative Review — Units 1–5

- **Unit 1** Write an *N* over each noun, a *V* over each verb, an *A* over each adjective, and a *P* over each pronoun in the following paragraph.

    A huge army of clay soldiers was discovered in China. People dug for water and found them. The soldiers were buried many years ago. An emperor ordered workers to build the army for his great tomb.

    (A huge(A) army(N) of clay(A) soldiers(N) was(V) discovered(V) in China(N). People(N) dug(V) for water(N) and found(V) them(P). The soldiers(N) were(V) buried(V) many(A) years(N) ago. An emperor(N) ordered(V) workers(N) to build(V) the army(N) for his(P) great(A) tomb(N).)

- **Unit 2** Circle the correct word in each sentence.

    1. Ski poles help skiers turn and keep **(their)** them balance.
    2. The long jump and high jump is **(are)** two decathlon events.
    3. We had went **(gone)** to see the Rockers play in Cleveland.
    4. Gymnasts has **(have)** very good balance.
    5. Golf and tennis **(aren't)** isn't contact sports.
    6. The pitcher wasn't throwing **(any)** no strikes.
    7. The referee had saw **(seen)** the foul.
    8. A football player wears a helmet to protect **(his)** him head.
    9. Miranda and **(I)** me like ice skating.
    10. Hockey is the more exciting **(most exciting)** sport at the Olympics.

- **Unit 3** Circle letters that should be capital letters. Write in punctuation marks where they belong.

    (d)ear Tony**,**

    I'm glad you got to see the **(e)**iffel **(t)**ower. Paris**,** **(f)**rance**,** must be fun to visit in **(a)**pril. Did you have a good time with **(a)**unt Veronica?

    Things will be different on Park **(s)**t**.** when you get back. Mr**.** and **(m)**rs**.** **(r)**amirez sold their house. We heard the new neighbors have three dogs, five cats**,** and a bird!

    I'll be at **(m)**idway **(a)**irport to pick you up at 4:15 p**.**m**.** on Apr**.** 30.

    (y)our cousin**,**
    Angela

UNIT 5: Reference Skills

Name _____

Cumulative Review

- Unit 4

Circle the letter that tells the best meaning of the bold word.

11. A border collie can **spring** into the air to catch a ball.

    (a). jump up   b. the season between winter and summer

12. Like some other **breeds**, this kind of pooch likes to work.

    a. dog owners   (b). type of dog

13. You should see them **round** up sheep.

    (a). to gather   b. shaped like a circle

- Unit 4

Write the correct word in each sentence. Choose from the words in parentheses.

14. An elephant is ___too___ big to keep as a pet. (to, too, two)

15. ___They're___ better off living in the wild. (there, their, they're)

- Unit 5

Write the following words in alphabetical order.

    crayon   candle   chart

16. ___candle, chart, crayon___

- Unit 5

Circle the letter of the correct answer.

17. Which source would tell you the forecast for tomorrow's weather?

    a. atlas   b. telephone book   c. dictionary   (d). newspaper

18. Which source would tell you how many apples to peel for a pie?

    (a). cookbook   b. encyclopedia   c. calendar   d. atlas

19. Which word is a main topic that includes the other words?

    a. circle   (b). shape   c. square   d. triangle

20. What part of a map tells you what the symbols mean?

    (a). key   b. compass rose   c. title   d. pictures

Count 1 point for each correct answer.   _____ My Score

70 Top Score

UNIT 5: Reference Skills

Objective: Students are assessed on their knowledge of reference skills.

Name _____

UNIT 5 Inventory

Put the following words in alphabetical order.   Lesson 61

farmer   field   hay   barn   hoe

1. _____barn_____
2. _____farmer_____
3. _____field_____
4. _____hay_____
5. _____hoe_____

Use the dictionary entry to answer the questions.   Lesson 62

sink (singk) 1. *v.* to drop to a lower level
2. *n.* a large bowl used for washing

6. Which meaning of *sink* best fits the following sentence? *The workers had to sink the poles deep into the ground.* _____number 1_____

7. Which set of words could be guide words for *sink: saddle/ship* or *sent/soak*? _____sent/soak_____

8. How many syllables does the word *sink* have? _____one_____

Choose the correct reference source for each question.   Lesson 63

calendar   map
newspaper   cookbook

9. Which of these would tell you how to make a birthday cake? _____cookbook_____

10. Which of these would tell you how to get to a birthday party at someone else's house? _____map_____

11. Which of these would tell you what day of the week your birthday is this year? _____calendar_____

12. Which of these would tell you about important events happening on your birthday? _____newspaper_____

Circle the letter of the correct answer.   Lessons 65, 66

13. Which word is a main topic that includes the other words?
    a. zipper
    b. button
    (c.) fastener
    d. snap

14. Which word is the best main topic for *knife, fork,* and *spoon*?
    a. plate
    (b.) tool
    c. meal
    d. food

15. What part of a map shows you which direction is north?
    (a.) compass rose
    b. title
    c. key
    d. streets

Count 1 point for each correct answer.

_____ My Score
15 Top Score

92

UNIT 6

Lesson 67

Objective: Students identify and write good beginning sentences.

Name _____

Linking Lessons: Lessons 68, 70, and 71 address supporting sentences, ending sentences, and sentence order.

Writing Structures

Opening Sentences

Before starting this unit, you may wish to give the Inventory on page 102 as a diagnostic test.

Rule	Example
A good **opening sentence** makes the reader wonder what will happen next and want to keep reading the story.	Shawna crept up the steps toward **the** locked door.
A poor opening sentence doesn't keep the reader's interest.	Shawna walked upstairs.

Write yes before each good opening sentence. Write no before each poor opening sentence.

__no__ 1. The lady put on her shoes.

__yes__ 2. The ballerina lost her balance as she leapt into the air.

__yes__ 3. Do you want to know the secret to being happy?

__no__ 4. A violin is a string instrument.

__no__ 5. A leaf fell from the tree.

__yes__ 6. A strange sound woke Mr. Shim in the middle of the night.

Use each group of words to write a good opening sentence.
Answers will vary. (2 points each)

7. the dog barked _____ Answers will vary.

8. Anissa dropped the _____

Extension
Look at some of your favorite books. Write down some good opening sentences to share with the class.

Count 1 point for each correct answer.

_____ My Score
10 Top Score

FYI: The English Department at San Jose State University hosts the annual Bulwer-Lytton Fiction Contest in which entrants must begin their stories with the phrase "It was a dark and stormy night..."

Objective: Students identify supporting sentences in a paragraph.

Lesson 68

UNIT 6: Writing Structures

Linking Lessons: You might find it helpful to review Lesson 65 on outlines. Lessons 67, 70, and 71 cover opening sentences, ending sentences, and sentence order.

Supporting Sentences

Rule
The first sentence of a paragraph tells the main idea. The sentences that follow it should explain or tell more about the main idea. These are called **supporting sentences**.

Example
Many inventions have made cooking food easier. **The first food mixer was made in 1910. People have been using pop-up toasters to quickly toast bread since 1927.**

Write yes or no to tell whether each sentence supports the main idea.

Main idea: The colors of roses have different meanings.

__yes__ 1. A yellow rose stands for joy.

__no__ 2. Rose petals are sometimes thrown at a wedding.

__yes__ 3. Pink roses can mean "thank you."

__yes__ 4. Give a red rose to tell someone you love him or her.

__no__ 5. A rose garden should have many different colors.

Main idea: Sacajawea was very helpful to Lewis and Clark's team of explorers.

__no__ 6. Sacajawea wanted to see her home again.

__yes__ 7. Sacajawea guided the explorers through mountains.

__no__ 8. Lewis and Clark named a river after Sacajawea.

__yes__ 9. Sacajawea was an interpreter for Lewis and Clark.

__yes__ 10. She also gathered and fixed plants to eat.

Count 1 point for each correct answer.

My Score _____

10 Top Score

Extension
Write three supporting sentences for the following main idea: *People do many different activities on weekends.*

FYI: Remind students of the outline they completed in Lesson 65. Tell them that the subtopics and details they filled in were like supporting sentences for the main topics.

Objective: Students identify and write sentences that stay on topic.

Lesson 69

UNIT 6: Writing Structures

Linking Lessons: You might find it helpful to review Lesson 68 on supporting sentences. Lessons 67, 70, and 71 cover opening sentences, ending sentences, and sentence order.

Staying on Topic

It's important for writers to **stay on topic** so that readers don't get confused or lose interest.

Rule

Every sentence in a paragraph should tell about one thing.

The sentence *We have a golden retriever* doesn't belong in this paragraph because it doesn't stay on the subject of musical instruments.

Example

Everyone in my family plays an instrument. Mom and Dad both play guitar, and Dad also plays the piano. We have a golden retriever. My sister plays the flute. We like spending time together making music.

Cross out the sentences that don't stay on topic.

The ways people tell time have changed over the years. Some clocks used by people long ago were shadow clocks and water clocks. ~~These people carried water in stone buckets.~~ Sand glasses, candle clocks, and oil clocks are other early forms of clocks. ~~Some beaches have white sand.~~ By 1300 mechanical clocks were being made. They kept better time than the clocks people used before. ~~Puppies like the sound of a ticking clock.~~ Clocks that use the mineral quartz were invented in 1929. ~~Talc is another mineral.~~ These clocks and watches keep very good time. Quartz clocks and watches are what most people use today. ~~My aunt got a new watch for her birthday.~~

Count 1 point for each correct answer.

_____ **My Score**
5 Top Score

Extension
Write a paragraph about the library with a good opening sentence and supporting sentences.

FYI: Some writers have trouble staying on topic because they try to include too many ideas in one paragraph. When a new idea is introduced, it's time to start a new paragraph.

Objective: Students identify and write good ending sentences.

Lesson 70

UNIT 6: Writing Structures

Linking Lessons: You might find it helpful to review Lessons 67–69 on opening sentences, supporting sentences, and staying on topic. Lesson 71 covers sentence order.

Ending Sentences

Rule	Example
An ending sentence should not begin a new idea. It should complete the main idea of the paragraph.	The Statue of Liberty was built in France from 1875 to 1884. It was a gift to the American people. In 1885, the statue was taken apart and shipped to the United States. The Statue of Liberty is closed on some holidays.
The ending sentence for this paragraph is not good. It should be replaced with an ending sentence that completes the main idea.	The statue was finally put together on Liberty Island in 1886.

Write yes or no to tell whether the sentence is a good ending sentence.

Yoshi Miyake is an artist who was born in Tokyo, Japan. She studied science in college, but she also liked art. After she graduated from college in Tokyo, she moved to Chicago and took classes at the American Academy of Art.

__yes__ 1. Ms. Miyake has illustrated many children's books.

__no__ 2. Priscilla Wu is a writer who has worked with Yoshi Miyake.

__yes__ 3. She opened an art gallery in Chicago called American West.

The action in a story is the story's plot. A good plot has a beginning, a middle, and an end. A story usually begins with some kind of problem. In the middle of the story, characters try to solve the problem.

__no__ 4. Plays have plots, too.

__yes__ 5. The end of the story tells how the problem was solved.

Count 1 point for each correct answer.

_____ My Score
5 Top Score

Extension
Write a paragraph with a good opening sentence, supporting sentences, and an ending sentence that completes the main idea.

FYI: The following terms are sometimes used at the beginning of an ending sentence: *finally, lastly, in conclusion,* and *to summarize.*

Objective: Students identify the correct order of sentences in a paragraph.

Name _____

Lesson 71

UNIT 6: Writing Structures

Linking Lessons: You might find it helpful to review Lessons 67–70 on opening sentences, supporting sentences, staying on topic, and ending sentences.

Sentence Order

> ### Example
> A writer should tell things in the order in which they happened. Using the right **sentence order** helps the reader understand the story.

Write numbers on the lines to show the correct order of the sentences.

__2__ First, they look in catalogs and decide what to order.

__4__ Then they sell the new pencils to other students.

__1__ Some students in New York run their own pencil business.

__3__ When the order comes in, they check to make sure they got everything.

__5__ After they sell the pencils, they count the money they made.

__4__ When you have an empty bottle or can, put it in the correct box.

__1__ Start a recycling plan to help protect the environment.

__5__ When the boxes are full, take them to a recycling center.

__2__ Get some boxes or plastic cartons to start with.

__3__ Label the boxes or cartons "Paper," "Plastic," "Metal," and "Glass."

Count 1 point for each correct answer.

_____ My Score
10 Top Score

Extension
Write instructions for how to make or do something. Be sure to keep your sentences in the right order.

FYI: In addition to time order, paragraphs are sometimes organized by place order or order of importance.

Objective: Students correctly combine subjects and objects in sentences.

Name _____

Lesson 72

UNIT 6: Writing Structures

Linking Lessons: You might find it helpful to review Lesson 13 on articles and Lessons 19–24 on subject-verb agreement.

Combining Sentences

Rule	Example
You can make short sentences sound better by **combining sentences.** When two subjects are doing the same thing, you can tell about them both in the same sentence.	Lilian Moore is a poet. Raymond Souster is a poet too. Lilian Moore and Raymond Souster are poets.
Other parts of sentences can be combined also.	Whitney Houston is a singer. Whitney Houston is an actress. Whitney Houston is a singer and an actress.

Rewrite each pair of sentences as one combined sentence.

1. Snails live in shells. Clams live in shells.
   Snails and clams live in shells.

2. The library is closed on Sunday. The bank is closed on Sunday.
   The library and bank are closed on Sunday.

3. Alma Flor Ada writes poems. Alma Flor Ada writes stories.
   Alma Flor Ada writes poems and stories.

4. Three is a prime number. Seven is a prime number.
   Three and seven are prime numbers.

5. Foxes eat frogs. Foxes eat birds.
   Foxes eat frogs and birds.

Count 1 point for each correct answer.

_____ My Score
5 Top Score

Extension
Combine the sentences to make one better sentence: *Aqua is a shade of blue. Cobalt is a shade of blue. Teal is a shade of blue.*

FYI: Remind students to check for subject-verb agreement when they combine sentences.

Objective: Students review writing structure, including opening, supporting, and ending sentences; staying on topic; sentence order; and combining sentences.

Name _____

Review Lessons 67–72

- **Write yes or no to tell whether each is a good beginning sentence.**

1. __no__ Jason picked a flower.

2. __yes__ How could everything go so wrong?

- **Write yes before each sentence that supports the main idea. Write no before each sentence that does not support the main idea.**

Main idea: People greet each other in different ways.

3. __yes__ Sometimes people shake hands when they meet.

4. __no__ Finger spelling is a kind of sign language.

- **Cross out the sentence that does not stay on topic.**

    Costumes are an important part of a play. ~~Noh is a form of Japanese theater.~~ They help show the time and place in which a play is set. They can even turn an actor into an object or a make-believe creature.

- **Circle the best ending sentence for the above paragraph.**

5. a. Finger puppets are easy to make.
   (b.) Costumes help make a play complete.

Write numbers on the lines to show the correct order of the sentences.

__1__ Members of Congress agreed on a place for the capital city.

__3__ A builder was hired to make plans for the buildings.

__2__ They decided it should be in the middle of the North and South.

Rewrite the sentences as one combined sentence.

6. Elephants are large mammals. Whales are large mammals.
   Elephants and whales are large mammals.

- Lesson 67
- Lesson 68
- Lesson 69
- Lesson 70
- Lesson 71
- Lesson 72

Count 1 point for each correct answer.   _____ My Score
                                             10 Top Score

UNIT 6: Writing Structures   99

Objective: Students review cumulatively Unit 1 (Grammar), Unit 2 (Usage), Unit 3 (Mechanics), Unit 4 (Vocabulary), Unit 5 (Reference Skills), and Unit 6 (Writing Structure).

Name _____

Cumulative Review — Units 1–6

- **Unit 1** — Write an **N** over the nouns, a **V** over the verbs, an **A** over the adjectives, and a **P** over the pronouns in the following paragraph.

    A N   V   N.   N   A   N   V P
    Many cereals contain wheat. Wheat and other grains give us
    A   N   N   P V   P   N   N
    important vitamins and minerals. They help our muscles, blood, nerves,
    N   N   V A
    bones, and teeth stay healthy.

- **Unit 2** — Circle the correct word in each sentence.

    1. Bread, pasta, and other foods is (are) made from flour.
    2. There isn't no (any) medal for fourth place at the Olympics.
    3. Sam and (I) me (saw) seen a manatee.
    4. Serena is the youngest (younger) of the two sisters.

- **Unit 3** — Circle letters that should be capital letters. Add punctuation marks.

    The Channel Tunnel runs undersea from Dover, (e)ngland, to a point near (c)alais, France. Building of the tunnel began on (d)ec. 1, 1987, on both sides of the (e)nglish Channel. The first train passed through the tunnel on Mar. 7, 1994. Colin (J.)-Kirkland wrote a book called <u>(e)ngineering the (c)hannel Tunnel</u>. In it, people who built the tunnel tell what it was like to make it possible to cross the English (c)hannel by boat, plane, or train.

- **Unit 4** — Circle the letter that tells the best meaning of the bold word.

    5. Clay pots and tools were some of the **artifacts** found in the ruins.
        (a). objects left behind   b. weapons
    6. We like to **coast** down the hill on our bikes.
        (a). glide or slide   b. land along the sea

- **Unit 4** — Circle the synonyms in the first row. Circle the antonyms in the second row.

    7. oven (mixer) kettle sink (blender)

- **Unit 6**
    8. (boring) tired short (exciting) hard

UNIT 6: Writing Structure

Name _____

Cumulative Review

- Unit 5 **Write the following words in alphabetical order.**
  9. turn   trunk   table   tire   thermos   talc

     table   talc   thermos   tire   trunk   turn

- Unit 5 **Circle the letter of the correct answer.**
  10. Which word is a main topic that includes the other words?
      a. relative   b. sister   c. father   d. grandmother
  11. Which source would tell you about the history of cars?
      a. cookbook   **b.** encyclopedia   c. calendar   d. atlas

  Rewrite the sentences as one combined sentence.
  12. West Virginia produces coal. West Virginia produces steel.
      West Virginia produces coal and steel.

- Unit 6 **Answer the following questions about the paragraph below.**

  Voluntary muscles are muscles you can control. Exercise helps keep a body healthy. These muscles help move your body. Your brain sends a message to the nerves. Then the muscle does what your brain tells it to do.

  13. Which sentence does not belong in the paragraph?
      Exercise helps keep a body healthy.

  14. Which sentence is the best ending sentence for the paragraph?
      a. Animals use voluntary muscles to find food and play.
      b. Involuntary muscles are controlled by different nerves.
      c. Voluntary muscles make it possible for you to do all sorts of movements.

Count 1 point for each correct answer.   _____ My Score
                                          60 Top Score

UNIT 6: Writing Structure

Objective: Students are assessed on their knowledge of writing structure.

Name _____

UNIT 6 Inventory

Write yes before each good beginning sentence and no before each poor beginning sentence.

Lesson 67

1. __yes__ The car screeched to a stop in front of the hospital.
2. __no__ My uncle rode a horse.
3. __yes__ This is going to be the greatest day ever!
4. __no__ What do you think?

Cross out the sentences that don't support the main topic. Lessons 68–69

Proteins are important to many parts of your body. Muscles, bones, and blood have protein in them. ~~Fats take longer to break down~~. Your body uses protein to build new muscles. Protein also helps to repair muscles if you get hurt. ~~Keep your skin healthy~~. Meat, eggs, tofu, and milk are good sources of protein. ~~Without water, you could not live~~.

Circle the letter of the best ending sentence for the above paragraph.

Lesson 70

5. ⓐ. Protein in your food helps you get strong and stay healthy.
   b. Fat also provides energy for your body.

Write numbers on the lines to show the correct order of the sentences.

Lesson 71

__2__ He called and ordered one with extra cheese.

__4__ Carson paid for the pizza and ate his dinner.

__1__ Carson was hungry for pizza.

__3__ The delivery person came in 20 minutes.

Rewrite each pair of sentences as one combined sentence. Lesson 72

6. Ginger is a spice. Nutmeg is a spice.
   Ginger and nutmeg are spices.

7. I put butter on my waffle. I put syrup on my waffle.
   I put butter and syrup on my waffle.

8. The book has a glossary. The book has an index.
   The book has a glossary and an index.

Count 1 point for each correct answer.

_____ My Score

15 Top Score

Review List

Mechanics

Use a **capital letter** for the word *I* and for each initial of a name.

Use a **capital letter** to begin
1. the first word of a sentence
2. each name of a person or pet
3. the name of a relative (*Mother, Uncle*) when used as a name or with a name but not with the words **my, our, your, his, her,** or **their**
4. a title of respect, such as **Dr., Mr., Miss, Mrs.,** or **Ms.**
5. a proper noun that names a particular place or thing
6. the name of a place and the name of a street
7. the name of a day of the week, a month, or a holiday
8. the first word and every important word in the title of a book or story

Use a **period** at the end of a sentence that tells something, after an initial, and after an abbreviation.

Use an **exclamation mark** after a sentence that shows surprise or excitement.

Use a **question mark** after a sentence that asks a question.

Use a **comma**
1. between the name of a city and the name of a state or country
2. between the day and year in a date
3. after the greeting and closing in a friendly letter
4. after each item in a series except the last item
5. to separate a quotation from the rest of a sentence

Use an **apostrophe** in a contraction where the letter or letters have been left out.

Use **quotation marks** before and after the exact words a speaker says.

Use a **colon** between the hour and minutes when writing the time.

Vocabulary

1. **Synonyms** are words that have similar meanings.
2. **Antonyms** are words that have opposite meanings.
3. **To** means "toward," **too** means "also" or "more than enough," and **two** is the number between one and three.
4. **There** means "at or in that place," **their** means "belonging to them," and **they're** means "they are."
5. The **context clues** in a sentence often can help you figure out the meaning of a word.

Grammar and Usage

Nouns

1. To form the **plural** of most nouns, add **-s** to the singular (*girl, girls*). For nouns ending in **s, x, z, ch,** or **sh,** add **-es** to the singular (*fox, foxes*). For nouns ending in **y** after a consonant, change the **y** to **i** and add **-es** (*sky, skies*). For some nouns ending in **f** or **fe,** change the **f** or **fe** to **v** and add **-es** (*half, halves;* but *chief, chiefs*).
2. To make a singular noun **possessive,** add an apostrophe plus **-s.**

Review List

3. To make a plural noun that ends in **s possessive**, add only an apostrophe. If the plural noun does not end in **s**, add an apostrophe plus **s** to make it possessive.

Pronouns
1. A **pronoun** takes the place of a noun. Some pronouns are **I, me, you, he, him, she, her, it, we, us, they, them, my, mine, your, his, her, its, ours,** and **their**.
2. Always **speak of yourself last** when you speak of yourself and others together.

Verbs
1. Use **am** with the word **I**.
2. Use **is, was, isn't, wasn't, doesn't, has,** and **hasn't** when talking about **one** person, place, or thing.
3. Use **are, were, aren't, don't, have,** and **haven't** when talking about **more than one** person, place, or thing.
4. Use **are** with the word **you**.
5. Use **have** and **haven't** with the words **you** and **I**.
6. Use **don't** with the words **you, I, they,** and **we**.
7. Use **came, saw, did, went, ran, ate,** and **gave** alone. Use helping verbs such as **has, have,** or **had** with **come, seen, done, gone, run, eaten,** and **given**.

Adjectives
1. An **adjective** describes a noun and tells which one, what kind, what color, and how many.
2. Add **-er** to most adjectives to compare two things (*tall, taller*). Use **more** plus the adjective for adjectives with two or more syllables.
3. Add **-est** to most adjectives to compare **more than two** things. Use **most** plus the adjective for most adjectives with two or more syllables.
4. **A, an,** and **the** are used before a noun. Use **a** before a word that begins with a consonant sound (a tree). Use **an** before a word that begins with a vowel sound (an orange). Use **the** before a particular person, place, thing, or idea (the smallest fish).

The **complete subject** includes all the words that tell who or what in a sentence. The **complete predicate** includes all the words that tell what the subject does, has, or is in a sentence.
Use **I** when you tell what you and someone else did or had.
Use **me** when you tell what someone else did to or for you and someone else.
When a **contraction** is made with the word **not**, the **o** is dropped (*is not, isn't*).
Use only one **negative word** to tell an idea.

United States Postal Service
State Abbreviations

Alabama	AL	Montana	MT
Alaska	AK	Nebraska	NE
Arizona	AZ	Nevada	NV
Arkansas	AR	New Hampshire	NH
California	CA	New Jersey	NJ
Colorado	CO	New Mexico	NM
Connecticut	CT	New York	NY
Delaware	DE	North Carolina	NC
District of Columbia	DC	North Dakota	ND
Florida	FL	Ohio	OH
Georgia	GA	Oklahoma	OK
Hawaii	HI	Oregon	OR
Idaho	ID	Pennsylvania	PA
Illinois	IL	Rhode Island	RI
Indiana	IN	South Carolina	SC
Iowa	IA	South Dakota	SD
Kansas	KS	Tennessee	TN
Kentucky	KY	Texas	TX
Louisiana	LA	Utah	UT
Maine	ME	Vermont	VT
Maryland	MD	Virginia	VA
Massachusetts	MA	Washington	WA
Michigan	MI	West Virginia	WV
Minnesota	MN	Wisconsin	WI
Mississippi	MS	Wyoming	WY
Missouri	MO		

A

a and *an*, 18
abbreviations, 61, 63-66
action verbs, 5
adjectives, 6
alphabetical order, 83, 84
antonyms, 76
apostrophes, 19, 27-30
articles, 18, 60
atlas, 85

C

capitalization, 49-58, 60-64, 66
combining sentences, 98
commas, 59, 64-68
common nouns, 50
comparing with adjectives, 44
complete sentences, 12
complete subject and predicate, 10
contractions, 19, 27-30

D

dictionary, usage, 84
double negatives, 43

E

encyclopedia, 85
ending sentences, 96
end marks, 8, 12
exclamation, 8, 12

F

fragment, sentence, 9

H

helping verbs, 30, 35-42
homophones, 77-78

I

index, 86
I or *me*, 23, 52
initials, 63
irregular verbs, 25-31, 34-42

M

map, reading, 88
multiple-meaning words, 74

N

nouns, 1-3, 50

O

object pronouns, 21, 23
opening sentences, 93
outlines, 87

P

past tense verbs, 26, 28, 33, 34-42
period, 8, 12, 13, 61, 63, 64, 66
plural nouns, 2
personal pronouns, 20-21
possessive nouns, 3
possessive pronouns, 22
predicate, 10, 11
present tense verbs, 25, 27, 29, 30, 32
pronouns, 4, 20-23
proper nouns, 1, 50-58

Q

question, 8, 12
question mark, 8, 12
quotation marks, 60, 68
quotations, 68

R

reference sources, 85
run-on sentences, 13

S

sentence order, 97
sentences, 8-13, 49, 73-74, 93-98
staying on topic, 95
subject, 10, 11, 20
subject pronouns, 20, 23
subject-verb agreement, 25-30
supporting sentences, 94
synonyms, 75

T

table of contents, 86
the, 18
there/their/they're, 78
to/too/two, 77

V

verbs, 5, 25-42

W

word meaning from context, 73